Die to Love

Die to Love
and
Awaken to Who You Really Are

Unmani Liza Hyde

BOOKS

Winchester, UK
Washington, USA

First published by O-Books, 2011
O-Books is an imprint of John Hunt Publishing Ltd., Laurel House, Station Approach,
Alresford, Hants, SO24 9JH, UK
office1@o-books.net
www.o-books.com

For distributor details and how to order please visit the 'Ordering' section on our website.

Text copyright: Unmani Liza Hyde 2010

ISBN: 978-1-84694-667-7

A CIP catalogue record for this book is available from the British Library.

Design: David Kerby

Printed in the UK by CPI Antony Rowe
Printed in the USA by Offset Paperback Mfrs, Inc

We operate a distinctive and ethical publishing philosophy in all
areas of our business, from our global network of authors to
production and worldwide distribution.

Love has never been spoken,
never been written,
never been imagined...

CONTENTS

Introduction	5
Longing	9
Lose it all	14
Who am I?	16
Me or Ego	20
The Nature of Thought	28
Broken Open	33
Surrender	37
Death	39
What is Love?	42
The Other	48
Intimacy	54
Polarity	58
Falling in Love	63
Relating in Love	66
The Madness of Love	71
Wild Sensuality	75
Unconditional Love and Compassion	79
Conditional Love	83
Hate	86
Gradual Dis-Integration	88
The Wrong Way Around!	91
Why Love Less Than Totally?	94

"There is an inner voice
You cannot even listen to
Because it is you…"

Kavita, Love Songs of the Undivided

Introduction

This book points to the truth of who You really are. If you have been genuinely searching and longing for Awakening or The Truth, then let this book point you to the truth of who you are.

This book is pointing to the end of the search. It is not yet another stepping stone on the path towards an elusive final goal. It does not give you any advice as to how to live or how to feel good. This message is ruthless compassion.

If you still want to feel good rather than know the truth, then this book is not for you. I am not trying to help you. If you read this book I will simply destroy you.

And who am I? I am you. I am Life itself. I am who you are beyond who you think you are or believe yourself to be. There is no separation between us, between reader and writer. Know this before you continue to turn the pages.

Know that what is written here, is written by you. You know this already. I am pointing to who you are beyond any idea of you who has decided to read this book for any particular reason. You have been playing as if you have forgotten who you are. This book is you gently reminding yourself. A friendly wave "Hello! Here I am!" All it takes is the courage to really acknowledge this.

It is easy to say that you want to discover the truth, but when you understand that the truth is not just the experience of love and peace, you may not be so sure that you want it any more. Recognizing who you really are will rob you of your deepest held ideas, beliefs, hopes, and dreams. It will turn your view of yourself and your life upside down.

You will either read this and find it unimaginably liberating, or you will find this extremely challenging indeed. No one response is right or wrong. It is the way it is. The message of this book is very radical, and not everyone is open to that right now. Perhaps, although you say that you want to discover the truth, you really enjoy the search far too much to actually find what you are searching for. What would you do without the spiritual search? What else could provide such addictive emotional highs and lows? Be honest. If this is not for you, close the book and put it down now.

So if you have continued reading, ask yourself if you are willing to die to know the truth? Nothing less will do. To know the Love that you are, you as you know yourself, your ego, will need to die. This is not the death of the body. This is a jump into the unknown. It is the last thing that you do, before you are no more. No more just testing the waters out of curiosity. No more playing with words and concepts.

True Love demands nothing less than full immersion. To die to Love is a complete surrender. It is truly realizing that no experience, no concept, no meaning, no state, no condition, no person can provide the peace that you long for. This is the end of all that. Haven't you had enough of running around trying to find a resting place, a permanent solution to all your problems and suffering? Give it all up and just rest now. Let it all go. Fall into not knowing anything. Never knowing. Never finding. Nothing to hold on to. Haven't you realized that you can't find the answer? You can never find the permanent peace and resting place that you seek.

You have been searching for a resting place in a world of phenomena which never rests. You have been searching to know who you really are in a world of endless identities. You have been searching in thought and imagination. You have been trying to know yourself in a life of endless reflections and meanings. There are so many questions and no real answers.

Haven't you noticed that as soon as you think you know something, or have it all worked out, something happens to show you that you don't, you know hardly anything at all? If you think you have the answer, soon someone will come along to tell you a better answer.

There is no end to these answers in thought. How long are you going to continue to fall for them? How long are you going to continue to believe thought rather than what you really know? How long are you going to continue to betray your true heartfelt knowing? This is the courage that I speak of – the courage to stand up for what you really know to be true, no matter what. This is what waking up really means. Waking up to who you really are.

Who you are is Life itself. Life living, breathing, being. But to try to locate, limit, know or identify Life is an endless search. Of course this is what everyone seems to be trying to do, in one form or another. People seem to feel more secure in the knowledge that they know what is going on, why things happen and how things work. Frustratingly, the source of Life or who you really are, cannot be found or understood in any way. Try to find who you are and you will only be frustrated. The paradox is, however, that Life plays at being known, limited, and identified. Life plays at being identified with this person here. I can say "I am…" or "I feel…" and I will be referring to this person right here. And yet, if I truly and honestly look to find who 'I' am, I can not find anyone. What a playful paradox!

You already know that you are not limited. You already know that you are not separate, that you are the whole – that you are Life itself.

Perhaps this knowing is felt as an underlying feeling that this is all a joke, or that we are all acting out a drama on a stage. Maybe it's a feeling of the purposelessness of it all, or of the ridiculous nature of everything that we do. However it is known, usually this knowing is overlooked in the search for something out there or some kind of special experience. This simple, child-like knowing is belittled in the face of the seriousness of real life. You go on searching or getting on with your life, ignoring the knowing which whispers the truth of who you really are. And so Life plays the paradoxical game of searching for itself.

When is it the right time to wake up from all of this? If you continue to believe that you are on a spiritual path then you will always believe that awakening is in the future sometime. You will continue to overlook the simplicity of what is right now.

Enough overlooking! It is time to wake up now, and know for yourself that you are the Love that you have only heard about. You are Love. You are Life.

It is time to listen to that inner Knowing.

This book undermines the assumptions that have been built up to protect you. See those walls crumble. It may be frightening, but wouldn't it be more frightening to live your whole life, without ever having listened to what you really truly know?

What is expressed here is not about the words. This is not a philosophy game. This is a matter of Life or Death. Until you get the joke, it is as serious as that. The words of this book could be analyzed endlessly, but this would be just another way of overlooking what these words are actually pointing to. The nature of thought is to compare this concept to other concepts and this word to other words. But this is not a heady, intellectual book. In fact this book is simply pointing to who You are in a way which jumps beyond intellect. Writer and reader become one. And in this union, the message of this book becomes obvious.

"Do not believe in a thing because you have read about it in a book. Do not believe in a thing because another man has said it was true. Do not believe in words because they are hallowed by tradition. Find out the truth for yourself... That is realization."

Swami Vivekananda

"To the seeker who is sincere, an experiential glimpse of this possibility is not enough. If you are sincere, you will find it within yourself to go far beyond any glimpse. You will find within your Self the courage to let go of the known and dive deeply into the unknown heart of a mystery that calls you only to itself."

Adyashanti

Longing

"Within you I lose myself. Without you I find myself
wanting to become lost again."
Unknown

When you really feel, you feel Love. Most deeply, most honestly you know that you are Love. Love is openness. This same openness is what everyone seems to be longing for. You are this Love. You are alive as Love. Your whole body longs to live open as Love.
Who you truly are is Love. This Love has no name. No shape. No form. Not even a feeling. It is what you already are without you needing to make any effort. You are Love. Love is unbound by condition, space or time. Love never knows what is next or why things happen. It is free. You are free. You are freedom itself.

But despite all this, you behave as if you are in a prison. Perhaps you believe that there is a problem and that something is missing. Or you feel you are not living fully enough. You suppress your true feelings and desires and have so many ideas of how you think you should feel or behave. Maybe you believe you are stuck in fixed patterns of behaviour. In an effort to create safety and protection in life and relationships, you may have built up imaginary walls which create tension in the body. Although sometimes these walls of protection seem to be useful, most of the time you long to break out and run naked screaming down the street! You long, to live without caring. To live freely in Love. To express whatever is in your heart. You long to surrender to the fullest passion of life. To feel and experience the Love that you know. You long to become as free as Love.

So what is this crazy dichotomy? You know, deep down, that you are Love, and yet you live as if you don't know that. Why would you do that? Why would you live as if you are restricted and limited when who You really are is limitless, boundless, overflowing Love? Of course we can give so many possible explanations for why Life would want to play this game of forgetting and then remembering. We could say that Life wants to experience or know itself and the only way to do that is by limiting itself to a particular aspect or part. This way Life can see itself as this person or this thing, whereas as limitless emptiness, Life can not experience itself. Whatever theory we come up with, all we really know is that, this is the way it is.

There is this dichotomy or paradox. Life plays at the game of forgetting itself, then longing and searching and finally finding itself to be that which was playing the whole game. In the remembering or realization of who You really are, you realize that there actually is never a dichotomy at all. Life is absolute Oneness. But until there is this recognition of Oneness, this play of believing in separation goes on. This is the longing.

This sense of separation or longing can be a very uncomfortable or painful sensation. There is often a feeling of restlessness and a trying to fill this never-ending hole with whatever seems to temporarily soothe the discomfort. This can be chocolate, alcohol, drugs, sex and even (or especially) spiritual books or practices. Various practices give you highs for a while, but then you come crashing down and the longing begins again. Perhaps you go on a peaceful retreat somewhere and have a beautiful experience, but then when you come back to regular life, the restlessness and feeling that something is missing, slowly starts creeping back in.

Some practices bring some clarity to a certain aspect of your life. Maybe you learn more about yourself and uncover more of the unconscious patterns which seem to weigh you down. But although this can feel temporarily freeing, as well as being fascinating and absorbing, there is really no end to the path of uncovering more and more about the story of you. The more you seem to uncover, the more there is. So while you continue to uncover more about who you think you are, you continue to long for who you know you are. In fact it seems that the search is driven by this uncomfortable, and yet quite addictive, sense of longing. This path of longing for more is so addictive because it involves those very juicy highs and those very dramatic and emotional lows. You are always chasing or running from something, you can never rest, and yet you say you are longing for peace and a resting place! Do you really want to find what you are looking for? Or will you just get bored and go off to chase the next high?

Haven't you noticed that no matter what high you experience or goal you attain, it always loses some of its sparkle once you attain it? Don't you really long for the end of all those dramatic highs and lows or imaginary future goals? Don't you really long for the end of it all? Death – what freedom, what a relief! What a strange thing to long for death. Unless you are very depressed and suicidal, it seems very unusual to long for death. But if you are really honest, that is what you long for. You long for the end of those highs and lows. To actually stop chasing and running. To stop totally.

This longing or feeling that something is missing, comes up in all areas of life, but longing for the perfect lover is probably the most common. You long for someone to complete you. You long to fall and dissolve into the other and know that there is nothing to be scared of and no reason to protect yourself any more. You long to know the absolute Love which has no reason to protect itself. No reason to play games. Nothing to think about. Nothing to wait for. No reason to do anything but Love. Right now, right here. Just Love for no reason. Just Love, despite all reasons.

However, no matter what you do, no matter how close you get to someone, no matter how romantic you are, however much you make love, you can never get close enough. You are always two separate people trying to get close. You will always feel separate and slightly frustrated. Something will always feel like it is missing.

This is the same as the search for spiritual enlightenment. You imagine that when you achieve your spiritual goal, that it will give you all the sense of completion and freedom that you long for. But whenever you experience anything close to it, it always seems just a little further out of reach. This search is never-ending.

But in falling in Love with someone or by having some kind of spiritual experience, you get a taste of the real Freedom and Love that You are. As you stare into your lover's eyes, perhaps you feel yourself falling and disappearing into them. For a moment, you become One beyond your two separate bodies. Perhaps in a meditation session, you have a moment where everything disappears and you are no more. Or maybe you are just walking down the street and suddenly there is only walking, with no one doing the walking. These kinds of moments can often be the seed which eventually can destroy your so-called normal life. Slowly things will start to crumble. Assumptions begin to be seen for what they really are. All that you have ever taken to mean anything starts to be seen as a façade.

Often after one of these moments or spiritual highs, while thought is quickly closing the gap which has appeared in its defences, there can be a sense that whatever that moment was, it was somehow special. It was somehow significant, although the mind has no idea what that significance really is. Thoughts try to hold on to the moment, but as soon as that happens, the moment has passed. You scramble around trying to recreate that moment in whatever way you can. You might try to recreate the context or situation in which the moment happened, but after some attempts, you realize that it is impossible. That moment has gone. You have lost it. Something is missing again and the search goes on.

Even though the search goes on, and the façade continues, you already know the freedom and true Love that you really are beyond all this. You already know that Life is already all so easy and effortless.

You already know, somehow, that you are not really a separate entity. But when there are ideas of a problem or that something is missing, these ideas are accompanied by such intense emotions or physical sensations and seem to be so overwhelming, that this knowing is overlooked.

At these times, there seems to be no freedom or love and only a feeling of separation and loneliness. There is only the limited perspective of negative, self-obsessive thoughts and beliefs. Deep down, you know that these thoughts do not actually mean anything, and yet they go on. You go on living as if you are in a prison, when underneath you know You are free. This dichotomy, or the sense that you are not living what You truly are, is where the longing for freedom lives. You long to live the freedom that you know You are already, and because you know this freedom, you can feel the difference when you live as if you are restricted and limited. You know that this can not be it. There must be something more... You long for that freedom, without realising that it is who you are already. You are freedom longing to be free!

Longing is actually an innate knowing of the true freedom or Love that you are right now, with the frustration that is felt when there is a denial of that. The denial is the restlessness and dissatisfaction with this simple moment right now.

This dissatisfaction with what is, is reflected in every aspect of society. Life is believed to be complicated and that all good experiences must be achieved through hard work and striving. It can not be that everything that you have ever desired is right here, right now.

Your mind cannot stand the simplicity of this present moment. It denies and belittles any kind of true knowing or recognition, that isn't scientifically proven, or written, and approved by someone else.

In fact, this tremendous longing is actually this true knowing or Love. Through this longing, the boundless depth of the Love which you are, is revealed. This feeling of longing is Love leading you (Love itself) to see that all there is is Love. This yearning for truth is not a problem to be solved, but a pull to surrender.

"We must see that we are afraid of the thing we most desire,
and so we live a mediocre life, never bringing to consummation
the primary impulse of our heart."
Unknown

Lose it all

"Many people come to the spiritual search looking for attainment, but true spiritual attainment is achieved through the conscious loss of everything. ....In the willingness to consciously lose all, the truth of one's being is revealed."
Gangaji

Before you can really know the Love that I am writing of, before you can recognize what I am pointing to, you have to lose it all. Otherwise, you will either toss it aside as a ridiculous concept, or you will say, "that's interesting but it doesn't do much for me". You might compare it to what someone else says, or just store it as interesting information.

It is very possible to hear this message and say "So what?" To hear it as an intellectual theory or philosophy, and either agree or disagree. You might even take it on as a new attitude or belief. But what I am pointing to is simply recognized or not. I am speaking of the end of all beliefs and attitudes. Losing all of them. Losing all reference points and all boundaries. Losing all hope that one day it will be better. Being totally and utterly left with nothing.

Awakening will not fit into your life as you imagine it or the self you imagine yourself to be. Love or Truth is not something that you integrate into your personal view of things. This is reality without your distorting stories, ideas, and beliefs. It is not hidden, but in plain view.

You have to lose all ideas of who you think you are before you can know who You truly are, and to value who You truly are. Lose all that you hold sacred and special. Lose all hope. Be totally left with now, this. Surrendered to what is. Stripped naked. No more maybes. No more what ifs. No more "someone else might know".

What does losing all hope mean? Any hope for a better moment than this moment. Any belief that some day life will be easier or better or that I will attain something one day.

When you have come to a point when you realize that there are no more possible avenues. When you have tried it all only to find that nothing gives you what you really want. When you have realized that anything that provides pleasure or happiness must also bring pain or sadness. When you see that any pleasure or pain is only temporary. When you have had enough of chasing pleasure and trying to avoid pain. The end of hope is really a readiness to die. A readiness to give it all up only to know the truth. To know the truth no matter whether it is going to bring pleasure or pain. Really ready to see that the answer does not lie in this world of phenomenon of pleasure or pain.

Losing it all means no longer trusting thought to know it all. Thought can think endless theories and can ask many questions, but none of them hold any real answers. Even experiences are seen to come and go and are not reliable. Pain, pleasure, pain, pleasure, pain, pleasure…. No more waiting for the end of pain and a permanent experience of pleasure.

This is the end of the search. In hitting rock bottom and seeing the pointlessness of it all, either when something traumatic happens or just from a weariness of searching for so long, then it is possible to hear this message.

This message is of the end of hope, but also of the beginning of Life. It is not a dry, depressing conceptual message, because in that emptiness, when all is lost, then there is the space to see the fullness of it all. The space to really know the Love that is, beyond any concept or fleeting experience of love.

Who am I?

"All that a guru can tell you is: 'My dear Sir, you are quite mistaken about yourself. You are not the person you take yourself to be.'" (443)
Nisargadata

Well, who are you? Do you really want to know? Or do you still want to hide behind who you think you are? What this book is really pointing to, is the true nature of who You are, beyond who you would like to be, or who you believe yourself to be. This is not always what you want to hear. This is not a pep talk to make you feel better. This is simply pointing to the reality. Are you ready to really grow up and know the way it really is? For better or for worse? Or do you want to go on living in a dream, hoping that one day things will get better?

Who are you right now? You have a name. But are you just a label? Who are you really? It takes some courage to really see who you are beyond labels and appearances. Are you a bunch of memories and a story of who you have been or who you would like to become? Are you limited to what you think or what others have told you? Are you really someone who has problems, needs, and desires? Or have you always known that somehow, no matter what happens in life, that things are really ok? Somehow you always know that life is not as complicated as we often make it out to be. That no matter how hard life appears to be at times, that actually it is all really so easy.

Beyond all labels and ideas, what you are is awareness itself. Aware of what ever is happening. Presence itself. Only ever present with no future or past. Timeless. Without reason or meaning. Meaninglessness beyond any idea of that being a depressing thought. Freedom beyond any idea or imagination. Freedom which is right now, which never needs to break free from any bonds. Absolute fulfilment which has always been fulfilled even when you were searching for fulfilment. Absolute wholeness even though you believe that there is something missing.

Simply what is happening right now. The sensation of breathing, the sounds of the cars going past, the visual image of this page... just as it is without any improvement needed.

The question then is, "how do I realize who I am without just believing these words?" Well, the answer is you don't. In the very recognition there is no separate 'you'. Recognize that you are simply a dream, an imagined figure who is believed to live in a story in time. While you believe yourself to be a separate 'me' you can not see that there is no 'me'. This very trying to do something is wrapped in the belief that 'you' are in control of your life.

This recognition is the bridge between believing in the separate character and the recognition that there is and has never been a separate character. Crossing this bridge is a death. This is beyond thought or belief. This is a realisation of who you are beyond who you think you are. If this is not recognized, these words are just words, and mean nothing more than concepts.

Throw out all concepts, just for one moment, and see what is left.

Throughout all the times that you have been seeking, did you ever wonder how you would be able to recognize fulfilment when you find it? If you don't know it, how can you find it? Or perhaps you do know it already....and then why are you looking for it! Can it be that you are looking to find confirmation of what you know already? Of course you know this already. It is most simple and obvious, so that when it is recognized there is often the thought "Oh that? But that's far too simple."

It is the most intimate and familiar. It has never not been. It is absolutely ordinary, and yet in this simple, intimate ordinariness, Life is no more overlooked. In this recognition Life is revealed as the miracle that it is and has always been.

Paradoxically, it seems that you as the appearance of a separate character, are touched by the experience of recognition. However, even this recognition is a dreamt experience in this story of time. It is experienced and then passes like any experience. Perhaps there is a blissed-out, timeless or transcendental experience, but then life goes on. This experience of recognition is the bridge between time and timelessness. Just for a moment in time it is seen that there is no time. Absolute insanity.

Life then goes on, and yet something is different. Something has been affected in a way that you cannot put your finger on. Nothing is different but at the same time everything has changed. No one owns this change. You cannot say, "I've got it now!" Because what have you got? Absolutely nothing.

The beauty of absolute timeless, limitless Life, is that it can not be held on to. It can not be owned. The owner is simply a dreamt character which will never actually own or achieve anything. You have lost everything. But you cannot even own this. You may label it awakening but what is recognized is never limited to a label or a concept of awakening or anything else. You may have experienced an altered state but even this can not be held on to. All experience and every state comes and goes. Nothing can ever be held on to. Nothing is permanent.

Recognize that no matter what the experience, who You are is the one who is noticing it all. Whether it is happiness or sadness, thought or no thought, separate character believed in or not, still you are. You are never really the separate character. It is a case of mistaken identity. You believe that you can fit yourself in a tiny box of a label of a name or role, when really

You are Life itself. Limitless, boundless already free right now.

"The source of the dream
Is ever- sparkling, clear, transparent
Electric, as a river unseen
Running through both dreamer
and dream –
I am kissed,
I am the kiss
Of awakening
To myself
From a dream
of separation
That never
Existed."

Kavita, Love Songs of the Undivided

'Me' or 'Ego'

"We do not see things as they really are, we see things as we are."
Talmud

Who do you think you are? 'Me'. What is this 'Me'? Who am I? Am I inside this body? Is this body 'mine'? Do 'I' own 'my' experience?

Or is there simply experience happening now? Right now, there is a visual image of hands on a keyboard. A sensation of sitting on a chair. A thought 'I am typing'. But who is this 'I'? Is there ever really someone doing the sitting or typing?

Or is there simply experience happening, not owned by anyone, just happening. Life happening right now as this experience, whatever it is. Sitting happening, typing happening – so simple.

And yet, paradoxically in daily life there seems to be an identity called 'me', who is constantly being referred to. This 'me' or 'ego' identity is assumed to inhabit a body and live on a timeline called 'my life'. 'Me' is assumed to be separate from other versions of you and is understood to have to negotiate its way through life.

Nature is assumed to be outside of 'me'. All sensation and experiences are assumed to be happening to 'me'. All this is believed in so strongly that when 'me' suffers, the suffering is a prison.

Many traditions teach that in order to put an end to suffering, you must transcend the ego or 'me'. But transcending the ego does not mean that it is gotten rid of. It is simply seen for what it is. The nature of this 'me' and the paradox of its illusion, is realized just the way it is. Just as there is simply sitting happening, there is ego happening...

In fact that that is trying get rid of the ego is the ego itself! What else would be arrogant enough to think that it can do such a thing? See the nature of the 'me' or ego. In recognizing the nature of the ego, it can be set free to be just as it is and is meant to be. So lets have a look at the nature of this 'me' or ego:

The 'me' is always limited to a separate body. Who you think you are is always limited to a particular location or a particular appearance. 'Me' can not understand how it is even possible to be all that is. 'Me' is assumed to be inside looking out at the world, having to negotiate, struggle to survive and prove 'myself' in a world which seems against 'me'. 'Me' only understands boundaries of inside and outside – separation.

If it is recognized that you are not inside a body, then it is very difficult to maintain a belief in a separate identity. The body is very much part of the identity of 'me'. But if you see that the body is simply an appearance happening right now, just as the chair is an appearance happening right now. It is only thought which claims the body as 'mine' or 'me'.

The 'me' is always in a power struggle – win or lose. Never win win. The nature of this 'me' is to protect 'myself'. To negotiate in this play of life and protect an individual called 'me'. 'Me' separates: Me, you, mine, yours, good for me, bad for me. Protecting against pain, or fear. Controlling, making everything appear safe. Putting limits with the idea that these limits will protect me. "I'd better not get too close to this person, because they could hurt me." "I'd better not show how I really feel because they may reject me".

'Me' speaks from fear, wanting to be safe, to know that personal needs are met and to feel in control. 'Me' sees the other as an enemy. Everything the other does, is perceived as a threat, every look, every word. 'Me' believes "I am not safe", "I am not loved (unless I am good)" and "I can control".

These beliefs are based in the basic belief in separation and fear: the belief that there really is a separate 'me'.

If there have been painful experiences of being treated badly or taken advantage of in the past, there may be even more tendency to try to limit or protect myself.

Thought seems to go around in circles repeating the same old patterns of pushing away or protecting myself from what is. The 'me' sees itself as a victim of reality. "This always happens to me." If there is hurt, the easiest thing is to blame. "My father/mother/lover hurt 'me'."

Thoughts tend to run along the same old habits which feel familiar and comfortable even if negative. We get used to our "poor me" stories. "Poor me, I always get treated this way." "Poor me, nobody understands me." "Poor me, nobody loves me."

What special 'poor me' stories they are. How special you feel. What a fantastically miserable identity you have!

The 'me' sees life as a struggle. There is the constant threat of hurt and rejection. It is constantly alert and ready to defend against any perceived attack. This 'me' longs to be appreciated, loved and feel special. It strives to relate and connect with other 'me's, but by its very nature, it only continues to maintain this illusion of separation. While there is a belief in a separate 'me' in here, there will no doubt be a belief in a separate 'you' out there.

Since feeling separate is often very painful, the 'me' develops well-practised strategies to try to feel safe and loved. These are often learnt from our parents or relatives or are survival mechanisms in response to our own childhood experiences. Like clinging to a relationship, being possessive, pretending that everything is fine even when actually you are scared or confused, hiding behind roles or masks, trying to be good.

These so-called psychological survival mechanisms do not really bring us love but instead are simply stories that solidify the sense of being a separate individual. 'Me' seeks approval and love from the so-called 'outside world'. "See me!" "Tell me how much I'm worth". 'Me' searches in this 'outside world' to know itself. It goes around feeling incomplete and searches for completion.

'Me' feels lost and is endlessly searching to control this feeling. Feeling separate and lonely and needing constant company or amusement, 'Me' does not know its own root in Love and Goodness. It reaches out, grasping for reassurance and attention. "I am not loved unless I am good".

But in this searching for Love, there is actually only a denial that this is already who you are. This can feel incredibly painful, but often no way out can be found. All that happens is a repeating of familiar, comfortable, but very painful patterns. In relationships, there is stagnation and safety. Love is only conditional. "I'll love you only if you love me", "I'll give to you, only if you give to me" – a power game of counting points. There is no real trust and surrender in Love.

'Me' does not know trust or surrender. 'Me' only wants to protect against the unknown danger. To keep everything known and defined. But although 'Me' proudly believes it is protecting someone, actually it is this very protecting that is the felt sense of separation. This very trying to keep everything safe and under control, is what keeps you feeling separate.

'Me' likes to correct, fix and improve just about everything and everyone. 'Me' continuously sees flaws and impurities, feeling superior and self-righteous as it points them out. 'Me' always forgives from a position of self-righteousness. You did something bad to me but I am big enough to forgive you.

'Me' is only capable of conditional love. Love for a reason and with conditions. 'Me' always separates and then longs to meet and become one. Love from me to you. Safe love, love within boundaries, and with rules. Love with ownership.

'Me' fits what we hear into what we think we already know and filters everything through that. The actions of the other are always seen through the filter of me and what the other means to me.
My actions are also seen through the filter of what the other will think of me and whether they will still love me. Nothing is fresh and new. This feels safe but unless there is an openness to what is happening right now, as if nothing like it ever happened before, Life feels dead and flat. So although this may feel safe, we often long for more. "There must be more than simply this routine, same old feeling or situation". Life feels stagnant, limited and simply miserable.

'Me' often explains uncomfortable or threatening situations or emotions away by being very clever and philosophical, keeping Life at a safe distance. This can happen with the cleverest or the most spiritual people.

'Me' is so tricky and hides so cleverly at every corner. By hiding behind beliefs or ideas, nothing is really allowed to touch you deeply and break you open. That would be too painful or too sensual or sexual. It might threaten everything that is so safe. It might bring down the whole house of cards.

You might then discover that no one is in control of anything and Life is simple overflowing with alive sensuality. In recognizing who You really are, there is no more a belief or a sense of a 'me' for whom Life is happening. There never was a real 'me', but while it was believed in, this belief acted as a filter for Life.

Life is experienced as happening to 'me' instead of just happening. In this recognition or Awakening, there is no more filter, and Life happens directly. Whatever is happening is simply happening in / as who I am. This is never known, controlled or understood and can feel uncomfortable and frightening, but it certainly feels alive.

It is the assumption and unexamined blind belief that this 'me' is actually separate, which seems to create the suffering. If this 'me' is taken to really mean something, then all my stories based in fear are believed to mean something and to really refer to a separate someone.

But take a moment to see if there is really someone to which this word 'me' actually refers. See that there is no one in there. Is this 'me' not just an assumption? Is it not just a word, a thought? Don't just believe what I am telling you, see this for yourself. If you do not find someone in there, then have the courage to really trust what you have found. You are the only authority to know this. Trust what you know to be true. The rest of society seems to believe in these separate me's but you can see for yourself that there is no me. Have the courage to stand up for this. This is the true rebellion.

And yet even if you do see that there is no actual me in there, there does seem to be a relating and behaving as if there is. In fact this me is the whole of Life only playing at being separate.

It is the focus of Life or Consciousness. The focus of attention on the experience of right now. There is seeing right now, there is hearing, touching, feeling right now – this is the focus. Believing that this focus implies that there is an actual separate me is what causes suffering.

The focus is never a problem. In fact it is an essential part of this play of separation. The focus or play as if there is a separate me is not bad or wrong – just limited. By its very nature, the focus is focussed on this experience and no other.

It is essential to function in this play of the world and a healthy sense of self is necessary for interaction with others. In knowing who you really are and understanding the nature of this me is allowed to function more freely in this play of Life. The me has a proper function: it lends focus to Consciousness.

It is like the tip of the pencil so that the pencil can write. The separate identity is the focus within the whole of Life. The identity enables Life to create and express itself. Yes, you are Consciousness itself, but, you are also you and not him, her or anything else. The energy of the me is fully honorable and justified in the energetic reality that is the play of Life. Awakening is the recognition that the me is also simply an aspect of this play of Life. 'Me' is who I really am only playing at being separate.

In this recognition, the ego is then free to be as it is. It can flourish and play out in a healthier manner. It is free to be the play of a separate identity because it is absolutely known that this is simply a play as if there is separation.

Generally there is a growing in self-confidence and ease. This is not the kind of arrogance you see in an inflated ego, but it is simply a trusting: Trusting that in not-knowing I know, trusting that the play of the separate 'me' is absolutely ok to be just as it is. Any kind of self-criticism or self-doubt is seen to be ridiculous and slowly seems to evaporate in the face of knowing that there is no one in control of anything. The separate character then becomes free to be more creative and expressive, to act spontaneously, to jump out of old habits and patterns, and to be more open in expressing what comes naturally.

It seems to take some courage to really trust that you know nothing. To trust in not-knowing, there is nothing to hold on to. So what is there to trust in? Only that you don't know. This is the vulnerability and innocence which is who You are. Have the courage to stand up for that. Have the courage to stand naked and trust that there is no one out there who can see you!

As Poonjaji said "Roar like a lion!"

This is really being ego-tistical, in the pure and neutral sense of the word. Although You are all of Life, paradoxically you are an ego, you are an individual. Feel how knowing who You really are empowers the appearance of a 'me' to flourish and shine.

The more you recognize that who you are is already all that you long for, the more Life seems to flow more naturally, in a way that is beyond any trying or forcing. It is simply noticed to be more of a natural flow with no-one standing in the way any more. No more apparent obstructions.

Who you are connects and relates beyond fear, is always safe, has no enemies and believes in no other. True safety does not come from the false sense of security of beliefs, but from knowing who You really are.

Who you really are is Love and in Love there is no me.

In Love, there is no separation. Love is only concerned with what is real and true. There is no more resistance to what is and so Love is all there is. Love is Presence. True Love loves what is. Love sees through any appearance of a separate 'me' and knows that it is simply a joke. Love does not recognize any conditions. Love simply loves and wants nothing in return. Love simply expresses itself as whatever is.

Love sees itself everywhere and loves what it sees. It does not have any opinion or preference. It does not doubt or criticize. Love does not discriminate. It does not believe that there is anything or anyone outside of Love. Love sees through the illusion of thought and belief. Love sees the pretence of a separate 'me' and loves that too. It knows there is no real separation but loves the play as if. Love does not resist or control. Love has no need to make everything safe. Love is never safe. Love is always alive and free. Always fresh. Always now. Love is a total surrender to what is.

"You have never seen the face of your ego, nor the face of your mind.
It is like a ghost, so as a ghost we accept it.
It has been handed down from generation to generation.
In reality the ego doesn't exist, the mind doesn't exist,
and samsara doesn't exist."
H.W. L Poonja (Papaji)

The Nature of Thought

*"A kiss is a lovely trick, designed by nature,
to stop words when speech becomes superfluous."*
Ingrid Bergmen

Often thought is seen as the enemy. In most spiritual or psychological practises we try to either change our thinking to be more positive, or analyse our thinking or we try to stop thinking altogether. Thought is seen to be the big problem that needs to be solved.

So often I hear people say "Oh my mind! If only my mind would just shut up!" But right now, are you thinking? No need to search for a thought. Are you thinking, literally right now as you read this word?

I am pointing to the fact that even though we assume that it is busy all the time, thought is often at rest. In fact thought is just as naturally at rest as it is in movement. Take a quiet moment to see, to look deeply for one moment; you may notice that right now there are no thoughts. Maybe just for a split second or maybe for longer, but in this silence of thought, the silence of who you really are beyond thought, is obvious. This silence is prior to any thought, including any thought about this silence. This silence contains a Love which devours who you think you are.

However, most of the time, the noise seems louder than the silence and the silence is seemingly overlooked or forgotten. This is why life can seem like such a struggle. Living through an overlay of thought.

Life is interpreted by thought and always seems to veil reality. Thought interprets, dreams, dramaticizes or rationalizes everything that happens. Thought makes everything seem like such a struggle or problem, such a drama. Thought can not stand ordinariness. If you meet a potential lover, thought will put in the background music and the fairy tale ending even before you sit down to dinner!

So how do you get beyond this veil of thought? The point is, that this question, this idea of a 'you' to go beyond thought, is all thought. Thought can not go beyond itself. Analyzing and trying to tame thought is simply an endless and frustrating game. See the nature of thought, just as it is, without trying to change anything. Already there is a relaxation in this natural acceptance of the way it is.

What is the nature of the mind? We make so many assumptions about this mind as if it is an actual entity. Is there a mind? There is a simple focussed consciousness. Perhaps take another moment to just look at the shape of this word on the page. Look at it so it is just the shape, the squiggle without any meaning. This is the simplicity of what I am pointing to. Thought is at rest and there is only seeing the word. This is the natural state of the focussed consciousness – empty of meaning, as if the word is seen for the first time. There is simply a focus on the experience of the image of the word.

Now go back to reading as normal and see that thought is doing a fantastic job of interpreting, analyzing or criticizing each word. It is also doing this fantastic job in this natural focussed consciousness. Consciousness is now focussed on the thought processes.

This focussed consciousness is often called 'mind'. It is assumed that mind or ego is the cause of all suffering. But actually this focussed consciousness does not cause anything. It is simply noticing. It is focussed on whatever is happening now, whether it is a physical sensation or a visual image, a sound or a thought.

I call it the 'focussed consciousness' because Life, which has no limits, plays at being limited to this focus.

Although this focus seems to shift from one thing to another, in this moment, you only know this experience and not any other. This focussed consciousness is not a separate entity, but simply a focus point appearing presently. It is this focus point which is often confused with the idea of a separate mind which thinks.

Actually if you notice, there is no separate mind thinking, there is simply this thought appearing presently in focus. Thought only plays in this very linear world of time. Thought decides what will happen based on what has happened. But beyond thought right now, there is no time.

Nothing has ever happened before or will ever happen again. Only this, right now. Right now if there is a thought, there is only this thought. There has never been a thought like it ever before. There are no such things as habits, patterns or conditioning. There is only this thought appearing right now.

If you believe you are stuck in these old thought patterns, stop right now and see the pattern for what it is – a thought appearing for the first time now. There has never been a past where you have repeated this behaviour endlessly and there will never be a future where you are stuck repeating this endlessly.

All that is left is right now, and this is freedom. There is no reason for there not to be joy and a lightness no matter what the circumstances are. Stop right now and see that this moment is all there is. This is the beginning and the end. Nothing has ever happened before this word on the page or this thought right now. If this is truly recognized, beyond any theory about 'being in the here and now', then any pattern that may appear to continue to come up, is seen for what it is – simply a thought happening right now.

See the nature of thought, as it is, not as it should be. All 'shoulds' only bring suffering. The idea of what 'should' be is basically dissatisfaction with what is.

As there is no escape from what is, this dissatisfaction is suffering. See that the nature of thought is to think things should be different and to be dissatisfied with what is. Notice how thought will always find a problem even when things seem to be fine.

Thought loves drama and action. Thought is movement and energy. When things are a little quiet and still, thought will find an itch to scratch or a problem to worry about. Thought can not relate to Absolute Presence. In thought Presence is simply an imagined concept. Actually recognizing Presence is a jump beyond thought into the unknown.

Thought does not need to understand everything. In life it seems that you rely on thought to conduct you most of the time. Thought is very useful. It helps define and classify everything so that you can live safely in the known. You walk into a room and almost unconsciously thought already has labelled this as 'my room', 'chair', 'bed' 'window'. How helpful! This means that you can walk into a room without worrying what all these strange objects are!

Thought is also very useful at trying to understand and analyse why and how things happen. You come up with theories about people, about life. If someone behaves in what you consider a strange way, you explain it as "they are doing this because they were abused, or they felt guilty or...." And again you feel safe and secure in the knowledge that you understand why and what is going on.

But it is in those moments of no thought when there is often the most creative inspiration, or moments of clarity. Thought can not understand, define or attempt to recreate these moments, and yet they happen. Although thought is very helpful, it is obvious that it is limited. Its nature is to label and explain everything to make it seem safe and secure.

Thought comes up with the most safe and secure assumption of all – 'me'. The assumption that there is someone in this body in control of 'my life' and what happens 'to me'.

Of course this safe assumption is reinforced by the whole of society. You go to a job interview and they ask you questions about yourself and how you might handle a situation. As if there is a someone who always reacts in the same way to similar situations. As if 'you' are fixed. You read a magazine at the dentist which has an article about how to motivate yourself or you go to a bookshop and see a row of books about self development.

Or even the words 'you' and 'me' which are used all the time in speech and writing. This assumption of 'me' claims every experience, every emotion, or every other thought as 'mine' or as having a meaning for 'me'. See the nature of this assumption, see that thought limits and restricts. This 'me' is just another thought which limits. Who You really are is never limited to a thought.

Thought does so much, but it is not the master that it is often believed to be. It is simply trying to help, trying to make everything safe and known, trying to understand. See the nature of thought, and see that it is only doing what it is meant to do. Nothing more and nothing less.

Thought longs to know and reflect the Love that You are in this play of appearances. Thought tries to do it all for you. But it can never truly know what is beyond itself.

Thought is of this play. Thought is the tool that Love uses to express itself in this play through the limits of appearances and experiences.

Knowing the nature of thought is to love and appreciate thought. It is limited, but it is not the enemy.

Broken Open

"Let the whole world break your heart every instant of the remainder of your life. Then this life can be lived in service to love."
Gangaji

What I am is absolute openness. I am not in need of protection. I cannot hide. I am totally broken open. I am pain, I am need, I am hurt, I am desire, I am absolute raw feeling.

I can't hold on to anything. It all passes through like sand through my fingers.

I am lost, so totally lost, without ever any hope of being found. As Life feels, I feel. Sometimes it overflows as sadness or pain, sometimes as joy.

Sometimes it is so overwhelming that it is almost as if this body cannot contain it all.

"I tremble. I shake. My tummy churns. I feel sick. My mouth is dry. My heart is racing. I'm scared. I act so tough. I act so in control and as if I have it all sorted. I act as if I know what I'm doing. I act as if I care about stuff. I act as if I don't care. I act as if I don't feel so lost and empty. I'm scared of being seen. I'm scared that I will be revealed as the farce that I am. Someone might actually see that I really don't know what I'm doing or who I'm supposed to be. Someone might show up the fact that I feel scared and lost. And if they see that, what can I do then? I will be open to be hurt. I will be unprotected. I might not be the tough image I imagine I appear to be. It might all fall apart. I might fall apart. I would be vulnerable."

These thoughts happen. These fears and physical sensations happen. But they are all happening in that that is already vulnerability. You can't hide it. You can't escape it. Life sees itself playing as if it could hide from itself. Absolute vulnerability is pretending to hide itself in itself from itself. Vulnerability is playing at being tough.

Vulnerability is playing at being able to protect itself.

I feel so vulnerable. I am unprotected. I am open to pain and hurt. And so I am open to joy. This sweet innocent vulnerability is what I am. I can not protect or hide it. Pain happens in this.

Joy happens in this. I am the openness in which all happens.

Life itself is like the hollow bamboo. All that happens, all that is felt passes through it. I cannot control any of it. I can't stop any of it. It simply passes through. Not inside this body. This body also passes through the hollow bamboo. Nothing to hold on to. Forever falling, falling. Never landing.

Absolutely lost, and then there is thought. A trying to find reference points. Something, anything to hold on to. Some kind of explanation or reason. Something to fill nothing. A trying to protect. This is the play of separation. You long to go beyond this play of separation and to stop protecting an illusory separate character.

Why does this protecting go on? The story that you might tell yourself is that others will hurt me if I do not protect myself. They might say or do things that seem to trigger pain or unpleasant sensations and thoughts.

Perhaps you have memories of past hurts which trigger defence mechanisms. Perhaps in the past when you have been open and vulnerable, you have been attacked and so now you have learnt to close up and hide your vulnerability. Perhaps you live in a society where other people all behave in that defensive way.

Whatever the reason, these protective mechanisms feel very familiar, comfortable and safe. And yet you long to break out of them and be free to love and trust and live as the Oneness that you know You truly are.

You become so used to hiding and protecting that you forget what you are even protecting. Others around you seem to be playing the same game and so it all seems to be perpetuated. Façade plays with façade. It all seems so controlled and stiff.

Don't you ever just want to scream and break it all open? Reveal something real? Reveal the pain beneath the fixed smiles. Reveal the insecurity beyond the pretence of security. The houses, the mortgages the marriages, the plans, the commitments, the boundaries and restrictions. They are no more than concepts, dreams, imagination, dreamt up in an attempt to protect the fact that really nothing is certain. Nothing is known.

You long to really be broken open and bleed. To lose control and to really feel and be alive. You long to live as if this is the last moment on earth. Like a child who screams when if feels discomfort and laughs in ecstasy when it feels joy.

You long to be that free and surrender totally to life, and yet you are terrified of it. Losing control or expressing joy is considered very undignified or crazy. You have so many ideas of what others may think. You have many ideas of what might happen if you really lived as the Innocence that you are.

Somehow there is still the misconception that by playing the protecting game, that this will really protect you. Who you are is always vulnerable. No matter how defensive and closed you behave, you still feel pain and suffering. In fact the protecting actually creates even more tension and contraction and in fact makes it worse. You may have noticed that if you have a physical pain, and then think about how bad it is and how much it hurts, the pain is exaggerated.

What are you protecting? The absolute innocence that you are, the innocence that you have always been? The timeless innocence that has not changed since you were a child and will never change or be in any way affected by however old you seem to become. This innocence is never touched by any behaviour, words or consequences. By its very nature, Innocence is untouched and never tainted in anyway. There is no need to and no way to protect Innocence.

No matter how much you pretend that everything is safe and secure and that you are in control, really you know that you don't know what the hell is going on. You have no idea of how to be. You have no idea of who you are. You don't know anything.

To recognize this is the surrender that you long for. I'm not suggesting that you stop making plans and promises, but know that no matter what you plan or promise, that life is still unknown. Never known.

"You can live in fear . . . or you can dance with her."
Unknown

Surrender

Whether it is to a god, or a guru, a teacher or a lover, we love to surrender totally. This is why the devotional path is so popular in some religions and cultures, and also becoming more popular in the West. We long to surrender. It does not matter to what or to whom, it is the very act of surrender which sacrifices all arrogance and separation to the altar of Life.

In the act of surrender the protecting game is exposed for what it is. In surrendering totally to a guru or to a lover, there is no inside and no outside, no guru or lover. In the total surrender, all that is left is Love.

We long to disappear or to lose ourselves completely and yet we also run from it in terror. If we surrender completely then we will lose all control, all limits and all identity. We are terrified of this possibility and yet we are exhausted with the effort of maintaining and defending a separate identity.

In Western culture usually we have too much pride to bow down and surrender to someone else. The word "surrender" is often interpreted as admitting defeat or being weak. But surrendering means falling into the total openness of who you are. This is not weak and is in no way any kind of defeat. This is recognising that you are life itself. Recognising that you have no boundaries, mental, emotional or physical, and knowing yourself as wide beyond any limiting sense of self you might have. No longer relying on thoughts, beliefs and assumptions. No longer finding any safety in what you think. Surrender is losing everything so that all that is left is Life happening presently.

Surrender is intimacy, vulnerability. Exposing that you don't know, and perhaps that you are really quite scared and lost. There is an absolute strength and power in that open vulnerability. Recognise the openness that seems to be covered up with ideas of who you think you are and who you pretend to be, and know that who you really are can never be hurt or undermined. You are life itself. Surrender is standing aside and no longer pretending to know it all and be in control. Standing aside and letting Life take you over and engulf you completely. Surrender means Love without limits. There is no one to defend or protect, there is only vulnerable, unhidden, and undefended Self. If there is pain there is pain, if the is joy there is joy, but no matter what happens, there is no barrier and no escape from what is. Surrender is sacrificing everything that you hold dear for this moment. Surrendering to the flow of the river and going wherever it takes you, no matter how much pain and suffering it might involve.

Whether thought agrees or not, there is an absolute in-loveness with what is, no matter what. Life doing you. This is Love.

Thought tries to do the surrender. This is not what I mean. You can not do this surrender. It is recognising the surrender that is already. Recognising that there is no 'you' here to do anything and see that this is already the surrender. This is already the Love. It is too late to try either to hold on or to surrender. Life is already absolute surrender right now. There is no god, guru, teacher or lover. There are no boundaries which separate you from anything or anyone else. Simply an in-loveness with what is.

All is lost. A dying into what is right now. This is surrender. What we call awakening is actually being touched so deeply by what is, that it destroys your life. Everything, without exception, is lost to right now.

Dare to let Life take you. Lose yourself and know what Love is.

Death

*"You are a player in this rigorous game of living . . . The first rule is:
every player dies; none knows when it's coming; the youngest and best
often go first. Everyone has to play. The game goes on forever - or until
you win. You win by finding death before it finds you. The prize – is life."*
Unknown

Game over....The end.... Stop.

Death is usually such a taboo. We seem to do everything we can to
avoid it. In our culture death is usually the most avoided, the most
denied. We are so terrified of it, so frightened of being nothing, of
not existing.

This body will die sometime; however, right now you have the
opportunity to meet death before the body dies, to recognize your
misidentification with the body.

It is the misidentification with the body that dies. And in this
dying, you wake up to the truth of who you really are.
Perhaps you fear not existing. In death 'you' do not exist. Many
have said, "But you are Existence." Believing this does not help you.
You have to know this for yourself.

Meet the fear of non-existence, and dive into the possibility of
your not existing. Who or what is it that will not exist? You do not
exist right now. Who do you think you are? Are you willing to die
right now, to be dead to who you were, dead to who you think you
are and dead to who you think you will be? Now, what remains?

Are You the body? Are You contained inside this bag of flesh
and bones? This is the normal assumption which usually goes
unquestioned.

This is the assumption of a separate identity which inhabits
a separate body. But if, right now, you investigate whether this

assumption is really the truth, what do you find?

Right now, are you not aware of the body? Isn't the body appearing right now in your awareness? Is not the sensation that is felt right now, appearing in this awareness? Trust what you find to be true. What I am pointing to is a total turn-around. See that you are not in the body, but the body is in you. This is the radical but simple truth.

In recognizing that you are not in the body, you recognize who you really are. Who You are is never contained, never limited to or by any body. Who you really are is never limited or affected in any way by whatever happens.

Who you are is always simply aware of this body, just as it is aware of whatever is happening. So if this body dies, do you die? Die right now. Know that you are not this body and know death right now.

Death is timelessness. The end of time. With the end of a belief in a separate identity, there is no time. See that nothing ever happened. There is only absolute Presence. No one left to notice the passing of time, no one left to remember what happened yesterday or hope for what might happen tomorrow. No one left at all.

Death is the beginning of life. Die to who you think you are and wake up to Life as you actually are.

This is Love. This is Freedom. The death of everything that has ever defined you. Death of all reference points. The willingness to be present with naked death reveals the absolute, undeniable beauty and presence of what is eternally alive. Meeting death right now is waking up to yourself as timeless Presence.

"Make me immortal with a kiss."
Christopher Marlowe

"A dream meditating on itself
Enters its own centre
And finds there is nothing there
But thin air
To face or efface…
Yesterday and tomorrow
Bow to each other
In the space
Where the seed
Of time's dance
Splits open…"
Kavita, Love Songs of the Undivided

What is Love?

"Love is clean. It is a searing fire of cleanliness. It is a sharp blade and it is fresh. It is so fresh you can smell it. It is like getting up in the morning at six and going out into nature. It is alive. The grass is singing. Everything is singing."
Bernie Prior

The word Love has been used ad nauseum, and that is partly because we can not understand it and partly because we know exactly what it is.

They say that Love is blind. I disagree. Love is Truth – absolutely all-seeing, absolutely aware and conscious knowing. Noticing all that is.

I am speaking of the Love which is who you really are. This is the 'You' who is aware of all that happens, and yet is never affected by what happens.

Love that loves itself despite it all. Love has no name. No shape. No form or even a feeling. Love is unbound by condition, space or time. Love never cares what is next or why things happen. Love is always fresh and new.

It is free – Freedom itself. But Love is also an annihilation. Love is the end of 'me'.

In Love there is no 'you' or 'me'. There is no mine and yours. All boundaries melt. Nothing to hold on to. True Love is a death. A death of all separation.

We have many ideas of what Love is. We think Love is lovey-dovey. We think Love is an emotional thing. We assume Love is outside of ourselves. We think Love comes and goes. We think that Love is the rush that you feel when you fall in love with someone.

But as soon as we think we know what Love is, we also know that it is not only that experience. Love is not confined to any one particular physical or emotional sensation.

Love is so much more. So much more that it is endless, limitless. You can never put your finger on it. Love can not be pinned down. It can not be known, because for it to be known it has to be limited.

Love is absolute Freedom.

Love is absolute Presence. It outshines all confusion or seriousness which seems to limit and restrict.

All ideas of who you are or what you think Love is, are simply burnt up in Love and seen to be meaningless.

You don't need to seek, find, or go out and get Love. You don't need to demand it from others, or even expect it. You can't get, seek, find, demand, or expect what you already are.

Love is already here. Everything is already infused with Love. You are already Love. Love is not an experience which can come and go. Love is who You are and this is the only constant, when everything else comes and goes.

There are moments when Love is recognized, such as when you fall in love with someone or when you are out in nature or look at the stars. It is in these moments that consciousness seems to open and expand as everything and all separateness is gone.

This natural movement towards openness is the expression of Love. In that expanded and open state, you know that you are Love.

You know, beyond logic, that you are not separate from what is seemingly outside of 'you'. But these moments can also feel very frightening and vulnerable, especially when you are so used to living behind walls of protection.

And so often follows the return to the more 'normal' contracted state of being wary of other people and afraid of life situations. These states of expansion and contraction come and go in this play of life. Expansion is when you recognize and experience yourself as Love and contraction is when you experience yourself as a separate individual.

This state of love comes and goes. It seems that you can fall in love with someone and then fall out of love again. You can like or dislike someone. This state of love comes and goes and seems to be able to be switched on and off.

You can choose to be loving or friendly towards some people and not others. You can decide who you like or dislike. You can have ideas of who you are not supposed to love and who you not should love. For example, you are supposed to love your family and not love someone who does not share the same beliefs. But the Love I am pointing to, is the Love that is unaffected by what you think or believe. This Love loves no matter what is happening, in fact, often despite what is happening.

When you recognize this Love which transcends all experience, then you recognize who you really are.

This plays out when you interact with other people, you know the deep connection which goes beyond whether you like or find them agreeable. This union is usually unspoken and yet is so much more powerful than the words spoken.

When this Love is recognized then openness meets openness. Two melt into one. There are no more boundaries – only absolute intimacy.

We know this so clearly in nature or with animals or babies, who do not seem to have a sense of a separate identity. We can easily feel at peace and love them. But when two adults interact, usually there are so many boundaries which are believed in. Two separate identities with such strong walls which protect and separate them. We are so wary of each other. But when these walls come down, even just for a moment, all there is, is Love. Perhaps it is just in a look or a smile, and suddenly there are no two people, there is only one Love. It could be with a stranger on the train, or with your best friend. Love does not depend on whether or not you know the other person or even like them.

In this play of Life there is a natural movement towards openness and truth. Once you begin to recognize that you are not separate, there is no end to this movement of Love. Love deepens and opens itself like a flower. There is no end to its flowering.

When there is a yearning for truth, this natural movement towards openness and truth is never-ending. It is continuously deepening and opening itself to Love. Wherever truth finds lies, the lies become such a contradiction that they can not last for long. You can not hold on to who you think you are, or any unconscious patterns, for long. Love tears down your whole house. You lose everything.

Love is Truth. Without the Love aspect, Truth is dead and meaningless. Without Love, Truth becomes an abstraction which is cool and analytical and this is not absolute Truth.

In absolute Truth there is a willingness to expose all lies, all beliefs and assumptions to this intimate connectedness with everything, which is Love. This is the willingness to lose it all.

Whether the personality likes it or not, an intimate connection with all that is, is there. Defences stand down naturally in the acknowledgement of the Love that is. Although thought does its best to hang on for dear life, more and more walls come crashing down, as beliefs and assumptions are seen for what they really are in the face of Love. This is the deepening. Forever expanding into everything.

There is often an expectation that this freedom or Love should be experienced as that, constantly. However, true freedom is not dependent on any experience of freedom. True Love is not dependent on being in a relationship or any experience of falling in love.

The Love that simply is, despite any experience or thought to the contrary, is the Love that you know you are right now. What a relief! You don't have to walk around with a permanent smile on your face or have blissful experiences, to know the bliss that is beyond any experience.

So when there is any feeling or experience of lack, it is known that it is not a real lack. When you have a problem or unpleasant emotion, you know that it is not really a problem because you know that who You truly are never has any problem. Who you are never lacks, despite any thought 'I lack'.

When you love someone, this is a playful expression of the Love that you are. One playing as two. One playing at meeting myself. Loving myself in this play of Life. And in this play of loving another, a 'me' meets a 'you' and they fall in love.

And yet often in this falling in Love is the recognition that the 'me' and the 'you' are not really separate. In Love all separation disappears. This is the Union, the Oneness that You are already. This is Love. The knowing beyond all appearances of a 'me' and a 'you', that there is only Love.

Love can never be understood because thought can never understand, what is limitless. The nature of thought is to limit, separate and to put labels on everything. That is its nature and it can not do anything else.

Thought tries endlessly to understand it all. To know it all. But Love is to not know. To fall into never knowing and disappear. No limits, no separation. What a contradiction! You spend so much time trying to understand what Love is and how it works and then Love comes like a tidal wave and destroys you!

Most of the time you behave as if you are afraid of Love. You prefer to play with all the words and concepts of Love, rather than face the actual annihilation of Love.

This fear is the separation that you long to go beyond. You long for Love, but you fear it because you know it is death. You long for it because you know that in dying, only then can you really live. You feel stifled by thought and concepts but often find no way out of it.

Thought tries to go beyond thought and so there is only circling in thought for years. In believing thought you live a half life. You compromise. You take life so seriously and believe that it is difficult. But beyond all that, somewhere deep down, you know that that is not so.

You know that it is really so simple. Right now, what can be serious? I mean literally right now. Reading this word. All that is happening is physical sensation of perhaps holding the book, or sitting on a chair. There is seeing of these words on the page. But that is all. It is really so simple. So easy.

Fear comes up because thought is threatened. In fact everything that you have ever known or believed in is threatened. In Love every thought, concept or belief is seen to be a joke. All that you have taken to be real and true is seen to be a dream floating in what You really are. All boundaries melt and disappear. All that is known is seen to be a safety net from falling into not-knowing. Absolute insecurity.

In recognizing the Love that You are, the reality underneath the overlay of thought is revealed in all its ordinary splendour. Love knows the beauty in all things, even if they appear ugly, painful or distorted. They are all part of this extra-ordinary play of ordinariness. An ordinary sound, a sensation, or a texture, is revealed to be extra-ordinary in its simplicity. Just the way it is.

A conversation with someone is seen to be a beautiful dance of energy. It is only thought that labels things as right or wrong or ugly or not good enough. Beyond thought it is all absolutely perfect just as it is. Even thought is seen to be fantastic. It imagines, it criticises, creates stories, it learns, it remembers...

Love is alive energy. Love is ever-morphing into whatever is right now. This sensation, this touch, this feeling, this is Love loving itself. Love is everywhere and is always here to be loved

Love loves itself and so all experience is loved just the way it is. Love is present awareness aware of itself and in Love with itself.

This is Love for the mere fact of existence itself. It isn't a Love that is caused by anything. It isn't based on whether you have a good day, or a good feeling. In fact, it could be not such a good day, or not such a good feeling, and still Love is. This is a Love that loves to live this Life because in Life it is actually meeting itself moment to moment.

"Love is but the discovery of ourselves in others, and the delight in the recognition."
Alexander Smit

The 'Other'

*"So dear I love him that with him, All deaths I could endure.
Without him, live no life."*
William Shakespeare, Romeo and Juliet

Who are you relating to? When you have a conversation with a friend or lover, or in fact with anyone in the street, who are you speaking to? Who are you assuming is inside the body appearing in front of you?

You hear them speak and assume that the sounds and words are coming from a separate entity inside a separate body. You assume that this separate entity has thoughts (probably about you!) and is relating to a separate entity inside your body. You see the space between the bodies and assume that the other is separate. You touch them and you don't feel their sensations but only your own.

All this reinforces the idea that this appearing play of separate entities is very real. In fact this play is so fascinating that most of the time we forget that actually this is simply a play. This is the play as if 'I' am separate to 'you'. As if I am confined to this body and you in that. But very occasionally, perhaps in a sweet moment of intimacy, we may get a glimpse beyond this play of separation and see that actually we have never been separate at all.

Just as who You really are is not confined to the limits of a body, so there is never actually another person confined to another body. Just as there is no one inside your body, there is no one inside the other. Instead there is the appearance of two bodies relating. Both bodies are appearing in who you are. Even though there seems to be a looking out of these eyes at the 'other', this looking out is appearing in you just as the other is appearing in you. This is not the you of the body or who you think you are, but the You that is eternal Love, the you that is Life itself.

In fact there is no other, just as there is no 'me'. You are absolutely alone. This is not the alone that is lonely (because that would need a me to miss a you) but alone in the sense that all that happens, happens in you.

You are Oneness. Wholeness beyond all appearing separation.

Without the other there is no me.

If you take a walk in the forest and are appreciating the beauty of the trees and sky, there is probably not much of a sense of a me relating to the trees. There are just trees. There is just walking. There is just a feeling of joy and beauty. But if you pass a person in the forest, or even just remember an interaction that you had with someone, immediately there is a you out there and a me in here. There are thoughts of shyness, trying to impress them, guilt, defence, what they might think of me and simply a general commentary about how 'I' am in relation to them.

Seeing the other makes me look at myself. Who am I? If the other is confident, am I so confident? If the other is friendly, am I friendly? In the eyes of the other, you see yourself, but this self is usually misunderstood to be the illusory me.

The very survival of the me depends on the existence of the other. In fact, that's exactly what makes the other so very significant. You love the other's approval, understanding, sympathy, attention, love because it reinforces your idea of who you think you are. Depending on what you see in the face of the other you know that you are a good person or a bad person. Without the assumed separate other, you have no idea of self.

In fact the most complicated and difficult times seem to be mostly being with other people. This is usually when you feel the most separate.

All kinds of emotions, thought patterns, pain and excitement are triggered. Protecting and defending thought mechanisms, and power struggles are triggered and this can feel very uncomfortable and lonely.

Often intense pleasure is experienced too, but then inevitably this passes and leaves a sense of loss in its wake.

It often feels like it would be a lot easier to live alone without any interaction with people. This is why some people on a spiritual path go away on retreats or live in caves or monasteries. Many people prefer the company of animals because they don't usually trigger such intense emotions as people.

That way they can seemingly avoid the suffering and feeling of separation that inevitably comes from interacting with people.

If concepts of separation are believed in you seem to suffer distance and alienation. You need to defend yourself all the time because the world seems very threatening. Just as there is the big experience of me in here, there is the constant assumption of the great big other out there.

Seeking to continually protect yourself you can not genuinely connect with others. You are too obsessed with me and myself. You try to reach out but you are so full of insecurity and belief that it will all go wrong that it inevitably does. In recognizing that there is no me it is seen that there is no other.

In other words there are no boundaries to cross in order to connect with the apparent other. Life is not solid and fixed. It is flowing and liquid. Constant change, transformation and flux which is interconnected and transparent. Each moment is new fresh. Nothing is stagnant or separate. Out of this knowing of Love, a play of connecting in Love arises.

In a relationship (between lovers, friends, family or even strangers) there is a play of energy that plays out. It is like a dance. Sometimes this dance includes intense feelings and pain. Buttons are pushed. Emotions are triggered. A position is held or defended.

A reaction, a projection.... Drama! But what is this all about?

When separation is really believed in, there seems to be a play of trying to protect or close off to the innocence and openness that You are. A play of trying not to expose the vulnerability that is really felt and known. So the games go on. Blame, guilt, victimizing, manipulation and more. These games and this trying to protect or close down is felt as a contraction and there is suffering.

Somehow it feels deeply wrong, even though in the moment it happens it feels like the only option. Over time, perhaps we get so used to closing off that this feeling of pain and wrong becomes a feeling we almost get used to. We blame the other and point the finger out there. This is the play of duality – right or wrong. Your fault. Not my fault. 'Me' is always right and feels stronger in blaming the other. Controlling and manipulating the other through its needs, demands or expectations.

Contorting itself to fit the other's image. But in the midst of all this, there may be an occasional moment of intimacy with Life (perhaps appearing as a lover or as a beautiful sunset).
The guard is let down and all the pain falls away. All there is is this. This moment. It feels so good in comparison. Such a relief. Such a feeling of expansion.

Then something changes and it is gone. These moments of intimacy or glimpses, are such a contrast to these thoughts and feelings of contraction and protecting. It is seen that the thoughts of protecting are somehow false and so the yearning for intimacy continues.

Even though this all goes on, You already are the intimacy and Love that you yearn for. Even though there is this play of trying to protect and defend, no matter how much this play is played out, who You are is still absolute Love. No matter how tough you pretend to be, who You really are is still absolute vulnerability. No matter how closed and contracted you feel, who you really are is still absolute open expansion. There is nothing you can do to disturb that in anyway. Who you are does not need protecting, but you cannot do anything to break down these patterns of protecting because the very idea of a you and a me is the protection pattern itself. You can not try to stop being separate, because the you who thinks they can do this, is the separation itself!

In recognizing this, it becomes obvious that there is no one to protect and no one to hide from. But even if the play of protecting goes on forever, who you really are is still absolute Love.

The voice of fear always leads away from Love. Fear is the primary mechanism sustaining the concept of the other. You fear losing control and falling into the other. You fear really seeing who You truly are in the eyes of the other.

In really recognizing that there is no other, you lose yourself completely. If there is no reference point here, there is no reference point there. If there is no identity in here, there is no identity out there. Absolutely alone, beyond alone – no one.

From a fearful perspective in thought, this understanding produces a desolate, frightening feeling. But from a recognition of who You really are, this is Freedom. Buddha said: "They abide in peace who do not abide anywhere". Nothing to hold on to. Lost it all.

Freedom to love arises from discovering that we can live without the concept of self and other. This is such a shift in perspective and can really change your life.

Love is not inside me or inside you. It is the very substance of us both. It can not be shared or given. It defies any appearance of separation. Any appearance of separate bodies. Love does not recognize separateness. It does not split itself in two. It does not see the other as the other. It only sees itself.

No matter what happens, there is nothing personal going on. This is true Love, a Love which is free of all boundaries and fear. To 'me', this idea of such uncontaminated Love, is unbearable in its intimacy.

When there are no clear separating boundaries and nothing to gain, the me becomes disinterested, angry, or frightened. In Love where there is no other, there is nowhere to hide, no one to control, and nothing to gain.

"Somewhere in a lonely bed of dreams
Before the dawn
One love rolled over
Into two
In order to
Embrace itself –
And broke
Its only
Heart"

Kavita, Love Songs of the Undivided

Intimacy

Just a look, just a touch and all worlds fall away. Melting into one. Falling into the other. Never been separate. Oneness beyond all appearances. All boundaries are meaningless. All concepts, ridiculous. No me, no you. No inside, no outside. Nothing means anything but this means everything.

It can be a momentary look between strangers on a train or a vulnerable, open conversation between friends. Looking into someone's eyes: "I recognize myself in you. I know you even though I don't know who you as who you think you are or who you pretend to be".

It has nothing to do with getting to know another person, and it is not necessarily to do with being physically close to someone. It is much more intangible, more subtle but can be much more powerful. In fact intimacy is the nature of Life.

As Zen master Dogen writes, "To be enlightened is to be intimate with all of life."

You can know intimacy with your cat, or with a leaf or even with the words on this page. Intimacy is to stand 'naked' with no boundaries or labels to protect or defend you from life totally consuming you. Love only seeing itself.

Recently, I was waiting at a train station to catch a train and I went to buy a cup of tea from a little tea shop. The old man who was serving the tea was reading his newspaper. When I said hello he looked up and gave me such an overwhelming smile, that I fell in love immediately. We just looked at each other and everything else fell away. I asked for a tea, which he made with such loving care, and then we both wished each other a good day. I got on my train with a smile.

This is one of so many such ordinary and yet absolutely extraordinary expressions of Love which simply can not help itself from overflowing.

In moments and tastes of intimacy there is no security. No comfort. Physically it can even be uncomfortable. But intense experiences of intimacy are often the most powerful experiences of Love that we ever feel.

In fact these moments are glimpses of the Oneness of who You are beyond all experiences. We could call these glimpses Love, Enlightenment or even Death. And that terrifies us. Intimacy essentially means death - the death of who you think you are. You fear intimacy because you fear losing yourself completely. Becoming totally consumed in the fire of Love. Merging into the other - falling in love so completely that your experience of separation from the other dissolves entirely and you disappear.

Have you noticed that some interactions with people are between who you think you are and you they think they are? Whereas some interactions are more intimate and open. They are lighter, freer, easier.

You know the difference but it is very difficult to define. Intimate moments have a certain flow to them. If it is with a lover, you move in a dance that you both seem to have been born for. It seems that you connect in a way that neither of you can understand but have no doubt about.

It can defy all rules, all restrictions. When it happens, you would be a fool to try to fight it with ideas of how things should or are supposed to be. The idea of a separate self simply stands to the side and takes a break from pretending to be in control and lets life just play. There are no longer two people, there is only life dancing.

While this may resonate, our underlying fear is that if we let down our guard and open to each other in intimacy – if we draw close and become vulnerable – we will get hurt. But getting hurt is part of this life experience.

The other side of pleasure is pain. You cannot have one without the other. There is no avoiding that, no matter how hard you try. You can hide behind words and concepts or you can avoid all sensual experiences in an attempt to avoid pain and suffering. You can have as many sexual experiences as possible to avoid being really vulnerable or you can defend yourself by never getting close to anyone.

You can take drugs to numb the pain. You can practise spiritual practices to overcome the agony. You can bury yourself in your job or in your mission, in order to suppress your desires and feelings. But really you still long to be destroyed by Love, by Life, by Death. You can run but you can never hide from the intimacy of Life!

Intimacy is life beyond separateness. The separateness is the belief in a me and a you. While there is this belief, there will always be a distance or a wall in between. This belief is the only wall.

Without this belief in separation, there is only intimacy. Life is intimacy. You are a raw open wound, open to whatever happens. There is no protection or defence. No one to protect or defend. This is a threat to who you think you are.

Who you think you are is safe. It is known. It is fixed and defined. You are a woman or a man. You are friendly. You are shy. You are a nice person. You like ice cream. All ideas of who you think you are act as barriers or limitations.

Intimacy is losing everything, losing all definitions and barriers which separate. All that is left is the dance of Life happening right now.

Sometimes the experience of intimacy can be so intense and revealing that often the first impulse is to run away in fear. It can be a terrifying experience when you realize - if only for a moment - that you are not who you think you are. All pretences are seen for what they are. All barriers come down and all that is left is vulnerability and innocence.

You are the innocent child, no matter how grown-up you pretend to be. You are pure Love no matter how cool and hard you pretend to be. You do not know, no matter how much you think you know and have it all under control. You are so lost and have nothing....You are absolutely nothing.

Although we are often irresistibly drawn to intimacy, we are also terrified and try to hide from it. We dance around it, longing for it but knowing that it will destroy us. We play hide and seek, longing to be really seen and pretending that we can really hide, like a child who covers their face and thinks that no one can see them.

Why are you hiding? Who are you trying to hide? Are you afraid that the façade of who you think you are will revealed as the joke that it is? You pretend that life is so secure and under control. While all the time you are trying so hard to hold it all together. Nothing must really touch you and break through that comfortable idea of who you are.

But isn't maintaining that façade so much effort? Don't you want to rest, to finally relax and put down your heavy load?

Polarity

"Love says "I am everything". Wisdom says "I am nothing".
Between the two, my life flows." (70)
Nisargadata

I don't know about you, but I have never really known what it means to be a woman. Obviously I appreciate that I have that which is usually referred to as a woman's body, but more than that I don't know what being a woman means. I have had many role models of women who appear to be very strong and know what to do or say, as well as various images in books or movies. But really I have no idea what a woman is meant to be like. I am told that I am a woman, but I really don't know what that means!

Throughout my life I have tried to find an identity that fits. Sometimes one identity seems to fit for a while until it is clearly revealed to be not quite enough. I have looked to other women to copy their self image or see what they think a woman should be like. But I have only found that there are a multitude of different images and so many women seem to be confused as to how they should be.

I have looked to men to see what they desire in a woman and have tried to be that. But of course men do not seem to have one consistent idea of how a woman should be either. No one seems to know how to be.

We all seem to be second guessing each other. Nobody knows what is right or wrong. I have tried to find my own self image, but then when I look, I don't find any self!

I do not actually find a consistent self image, no matter how hard I look. The expression as this woman is ever changing, absolutely freshly appearing right now.

Men and women are strange creatures. They don't fit into boxes which define them easily. Thought can see tendencies and similarities and then pronounces all men to be like this or all women to be like that. Sometimes this seems to be true, but really there are no men or women, there are no tendencies or similarities. It only seems that way while it conveniently fits into a theory or comparison thought.

The truth is that we just don't know the best or right way to be. We flounder through life never knowing, while thought tries to help out by labelling and defining and explaining it all so that it seems safe and known.

What I really am has no gender and no quality. I am formless. I am absolutely One beyond any idea of separation, and yet paradoxically, there is an appearing separate form. This is the paradox that is at the root of all mysteries. This is the mystery of Love. It is the meeting of the two aspects of this paradox that is the true falling in Love.

The Form and the Formless meet right now as One and the same. The Form recognizing that there is only the Formless appearing as Form. No-separation playing at being separate. Wholeness playing at being parts.

Aliveness and Emptiness. Love and Freedom. Personal and impersonal.

We could call this the dance between the male and female energies, but that seems to get too complicated. It is nothing to do with whether you are a man or a woman or your sexuality. The true meeting goes beyond any question of gender or sexuality. This does not even require someone else to fall in love with (although the expression of loving another is a reflection of this paradox). The Form and Formless are not limited to a particular body or energy. Formlessness plays as the individual form, and in this play the individual can recognize their Formless nature. In this timeless moment of recognition, there is no longer any Form, only Formlessness. And yet, the play of Form goes on... The individual goes on appearing and behaving as if it is separate, but knowing all the while that there is never any separation.

Throughout history and society today, there is confusion about how these aspects are actually already balanced and not separate. In many spiritual beliefs and traditions, there has been a tendency to believe that one must transcend the Form or go beyond separation to a higher plane. But this life is the play of unity, and separation, as one. There is no need or no way to transcend the Form, just see that the Form is the Formless already.

The Tao yin-yang symbol demonstrates the true situation very well. In the Form, there is always a core of the Formless, and in the Formless a core of the Form, just as there is a white dot in the black and a black dot in the white. But it seems that this mystical unity of the Form and Formless is often forgotten and instead these aspects are understood as being truly separate and limited to male and female. The absolute unity is often overlooked. There is not one without the other. Female, male, Form, Formlessness, Life, Death are one.

It seems that so often these paradoxical two aspects of the One, are misunderstood in the search for and playing out of personal identity. There can be a chaotic, personalized emotion (usually associated with woman) or a distant and impersonal detachment (usually associated with man). The chaotic personalized emotion fears the impersonal as being cold and unloving, whereas the impersonal detachment fears the personal emotion as being too fiery and vulnerable.

But without the clarity of the impersonal, we become too self-obsessed to be able to see clearly, and without being fiery and vulnerable we are also unable to love and feel truly alive.

Although one is irresistibly attracted to the other, both aspects resist and fear the other. They know the very real danger of losing themselves in the other. There is the longing for the balance of the two aspects. There is a sense of incompletion without it. Fire and ice. Yin and Yang. The fiery chaotic personalized emotion longs for clarity and focus, while the icy impersonal disassociation longs to be broken open and feel and express. But there is no real balance through a trying to modify behaviour or thought, this is only an endless uphill struggle.

Only in the recognition of the Oneness that You are beyond any idea of personal or impersonal, is Form known to be Formless and the Formless is known in the Form. This is the natural balance.

Formlessness, which we could also call Freedom, is pure Being. It is all encompassing and oceanic and does not differentiate or individualize. It is stillness, silence. It is limitless and boundless. It is literally empty nothingness. Absence. It is impersonal Oneness. It is death.

However, if you do not truly understand the nature of this aspect, you will only fear and paradoxically desire it. You will negate it, exploit it, try to get it. You are either lusting for it or turning from it, in every moment, unless there is an absolute recognition that this is Your nature already and that there is no escape from it. Who You are is absolute Formless Freedom.

The Form, which we could also call Love, is the play of appearing Life. It is absolute sensuality. It is movement. It is the fullness, the richness of life as it is. Presence.

Whatever the Form is, it is overflowing with Life. It is the play as if there are limits and separate individuals and objects. There are endless appearances, experiences and sensations, feelings, thoughts... Whatever happens, no matter how subtle, is Life overflowing with Love. But if you do not truly understand this aspect you will live as if these forms are flat and lifeless. You will not appreciate the Love that is in whatever happens. Your true nature is absolute Love.

It is only for the sake of words, which naturally do separate and limit, that these are expressed as two. These two aspects can not really be separated as they are not really two. The Formless is the Form and the Form is the Formless. Empty, limitless Freedom expresses itself as the fullness and love of this happening right now. Stillness is in movement. Movement is Stillness moving. Freedom and Love are one and the same. If this is recognized, this is known beyond all words which try to define this. This is known beyond all concepts of Yin and Yang, male and female, Life and Death.

It is amusing to look at the words: I AM. In this, precisely those two aspects merge. The 'I' is separating, differentiating, it gives focus, it gives direction, it individuates: I, not the other, I. And then 'AM'. AM is oceanic, all encompassing; it reflects the ocean of the One, the limitless Being that knows no bounds, no differentiation. In the I AM, these are both One.

Recognition of, or waking up to your true nature, is when Form recognizes itself as Formlessness and they fall into each other. Then there is no more separation. The Form is known to be the Formless. Then there is no going back. This is true intimacy, true Love. This is Love loving itself. Life living itself. The dreamer waking up in the dream and recognizing that it is a dream. Life is experienced fully, in all its natural and sensual glory.

This is transcending all polarities of male or female, life and death. In fact they are not really transcended, they are dived into.

"I am my beloved, and my beloved is me."
Song of Solomon

Falling in Love

"Out beyond wrongdoing and rightdoing there is a field.
I'll meet you there. When the soul lies down in that grass,
the world is too full to talk about. Ideas, language, even the
phrase 'each other' doesn't make any sense."
Rumi

Falling in love is played out like the best Hollywood movie. We are such good actors and actresses. A dramatic play on a stage. A play. A play as if it is all real. A play as if there really is a you and me. A play as if we fall in love like in the actual movies. A play as if we fall out of love and as if I get sad and miss you. Love watching itself play as two separate individuals loving each other. Two individuals playing at meeting as if they were able to ever really meet.

Haven't you noticed that no matter how close you get to someone, you never actually get close enough? You can never merge and be one. This is a play of separation. It is supposed to be like that. As separate individuals you will never meet.

But in this matrix of separation there are some glitches, moments when the movie is seen for what it is and the experience is of no separation. Two individuals melt into one in Love. In Love there are no two people, there is just Love. These glitches are moments which directly point to who You are beyond who you think you are most of the time.

"I have always been waiting for someone. That very special someone who will come into my life and sweep me off my feet. He will be the perfect one for me. He will understand me completely and complement me in everyway. He will bring me fulfilment and make all the pain go away."

This is apparently called falling in love, the final solution to all suffering. Searching for fulfilment in relationships is just like searching for enlightenment in spiritual practices or for peace through therapy. It is all based in the belief in a lack, a belief that something is missing in my life. "If only I would find the perfect person who would really truly understand me, then everything would be fine."

This is of course reinforced everywhere we look in films, love stories, music, poetry... We dream about a prince charming or a beautiful princess. We dream about the perfect relationship and a happy ever-after ending.

But beyond the fantasy of falling in love with the perfect person, what is it that you really long for in falling in love? Completion, oneness, a sense of wholeness – Love. You simply long to love totally. To surrender totally to the other in love that is not dependent on the physical and emotional sensations.

You long to be touched so deeply that you are cut open and bleed. You long to really feel alive with all the intensity that that means. You long to really be met, and be seen for who you really are and to love and be loved just the way you are. You long to be openly vulnerable with another and for that to be safe and loved. But when there is a belief that someone else must fulfil this longing, this is a delusion and inevitably leads to dependency, addiction and suffering.

No one else can make you feel whole because you are already whole just as you are. In any moment you believe you are only a fragment of Love rather than the whole, then you begin to yearn for the boundless Love that you really are.

When you dream and fantasize that you will one day find someone to complete you, or when you expect your lover to make you feel whole, you are actually reinforcing the belief that you are not already whole.

Love is not about someone outside of me, but a knowing of the Love that I am. This is reflected in the love between two people – in other words, I meet the Love that I am. It appears to have a face but truly it is faceless, and what I recognize and love is the facelessness of Love.

That is eternal Love. In fact there is no distinction between experience and beyond that. No separation from what is within and without. Love loves itself.

Therefore there is no need to be in love with someone else, in order to feel complete and whole. There is no need to be in love with someone else in order to be in love. Love is who You are.

Recognize this and then relating with a lover becomes a beautiful play of intimacy with Life, without the pressure of it needing to fulfil you. When there is no longer a belief that there is anyone to hide from, there is no reason not to be vulnerable and intimate with the other. If you recognize that You are Love, there is no reason not to love the other totally.

Love plays at being separate and then at meeting. Relating in Love means not referring to the other as who you think they are or who they think they are, but instead referring to the other as the Love that You are beyond appearances. Relating beyond separation.

Love loves to see itself and bathe in itself. There is always a particular flavour to a meeting beyond thought, when Love recognizes itself in the other and all there is is a play of energy. Love dancing as Life energy. Not imagining that the other is anything other than the Love that is. In loving the other, the Love that you are is revealed in all its splendour.

Beyond words or appearances, it is obvious that nothing is ever actually separate. In seeing this, that is, seeing the play of separation for what it really is, a play of Love, then there is a lightness to every meeting.

This is fearless relating. Love loving even fear. Something in you recognizes Love. It is not a movement of mind, or of understanding, it is a direct recognition of that that You are. It is a direct communication, a direct remembering beyond all appearances, of who You are.

"What would life be without love?
How peaceful, how tranquil and how dull!"
Lyric from a song I once heard.

Relating in Love

"Stand aside. There is no space for 'you' in Love.
Let go and fall into the other."
Unknown

Feeling dizzy, silly and light. Lost all control. Floaty, flighty, blissful losing everything but the one you love. You can be in a room full of people and feel that actually there is only the beloved. He fills you. There is nothing left but him.

Chemistry. So strong. So overwhelming and nowhere to hide from it. Overpowering intimacy. Feeling more alive than any other time.

Longing, yearning to dissolve any distance, any barrier. Longing to melt all icicles. Everything else disappears into oblivion. Such a high, such adrenalin pumping through the body, swept away with it. Loss of control. Falling into it. No way out. Loves overwhelms. All encompassing. I love it! I love being in love!

We love to be in love because we long for confirmation of what we know. In the eyes of the other, you know yourself. You long to look into the eyes of the other and be met, to be known for who you truly are.

This is what I mean, to be destroyed. In this moment of true meeting, the attention is brought so forcibly to the present with a jolt that is terrifying but thrilling. You lose everything that ever meant anything. Nothing is more important than this. This is everything you long for. This is death and yet this is the most alive you can feel.

The body is overwhelmed with intense sensations, the mind is absolutely silent. There is a simple resting in who you are as it is recognized in the other.

Then perhaps a moment or two later, the mind begins to scramble around trying to understand what has happened. It explains it by saying that this person is the one, or we should get married and promise to stay together forever, or perhaps thought gets so terrified by this death of separation between two people, that it wants to run a mile!

But it is only a game. We are only pretending to be separate. We play at longing to reunite as one, as if we are really separate. What a ridiculous but delicious game! We both know that it is all a pretence. We hide and play our roles so well. We pretend so well that we even seem to forget that we are Love itself.

You spend your life as if you are alone in a world full of strangers. As if no one truly loves you. Longing for the perfect lover to take away the pain of separation. But no matter how fearful and separated you feel, no matter how wary of others you feel, you still know that the other is somehow a key to total surrender. Being with the other seems to be the cause of so much suffering. So much protecting and defending of an illusory separate self.

Intimate relationships seem to be the one area which throws all states of peace or enlightenment into disarray. When faced with the other there is either an expression of fear or love. Hold on or surrender. Believe in separation or know that they are who you are. There is no particular kind of relating which is better or worse or right or wrong. Life takes its course no matter what you think or decide anyway. No theory or idea about relationships works for everyone. Some people play the game of commitment and marriage, some play the game of many partners. It seems to work out well when two people enjoy playing the same game!

We love when love is reflected back from the one we relate to. When there are clearly no boundaries of separation. Love loving itself. Some relating is like this and some is a dance in words and thought. Sometimes there is fear of the other.

Sometimes it is a game of hide and seek and sometimes it is a dance of intimate lovers. Many people seem to stay in a relationship where they play out their worst fears and some are in a relationship where they play out their greatest desires.

Whatever the game, a relationship seems to be a great opportunity to see the fears for what they are, as well as the reflections of who we believe ourselves to be. It is also a beautiful opportunity to know the vulnerability that Love is, despite everything else that plays out.

A relationship can be an annihilation. No matter how tough you think you are, no matter how in control you think you are, no matter how enlightened you think you are, relating in love can totally destroy all that. You are truly faced with some very intense emotions and sensations, some of which are very enjoyable and most of which are extremely uncomfortable.

All logic, all sense of control and order is burnt in the fire. You are ripped open and at the mercy of Love, as thought tries desperately to maintain some kind of decorum amongst the chaos. There is no way to navigate in this. There is no compass which can work in this terrain. Thought is seen to be a ridiculous attempt to hold back the tide.

A relationship is never really a relationship. A relationship is like being in an intensive opening the heart therapy workshop! All of mind's most defensive stories and dramas are played out, every method possible to try to maintain a sense of control and identity. A relationship is often so uncomfortable because of this fact.

It is a dance of separation versus Oneness. One playing at two. Melting into One and then desperately struggling to be separate again. All boundaries disappear and everything is perfect, and then thought comes in and says "Yes, but....you didn't make the bed!"

It is Life's most beautiful game.

In falling in love there is a recognition of the Love that You are. This Love never comes or goes, although all the stories and dramas come and go. Love is absolutely permanent. When you fall in love with someone, you recognize the Love that you are, even though at the time you may believe that it is dependent on the one you love. It is never about the other. It is only about you.

As a good male friend of mine said to the woman he was

trying to entice into intimacy, "A relationship with me is actually a relationship with yourself". Apart from this being a very good chat-up line, it is also true.

Know that the other is yourself and then when conflict and ideas of separation arise there is a natural loving despite this. By relating to the other as the Love that you are rather than a separate identity, the identity has less and less of a place to stand. Love despite conflict. Love despite an appearing separate identity.

A relationship is not ever really a relationship between two people, it is a dance of Love. Loving yourself in another. Loving for Love's sake. And in this beautiful and terrible, intricate, insane, wild, serene ballet there can be ecstasy and agony. Ups and downs both feel so intensely alive. What goes up must come down. It is inevitable. If you experience ecstasy, you will no doubt experience agony. There is no way out of that.

This the dance of Life, waves of energy which play out as attraction, repulsion, contraction, expansion. Sometimes there is a free flow of love and sometimes there are feelings of irritation. Sometimes there is a wanting to be together and sometimes a wanting to be apart. Sometimes a wanting to love and sometimes a wanting to fight.

The appearing other is human with all the frailties and limits of that. They can not always be happy and loving. They can not always do what you want. They can not always agree with you. They do not fit into a neat concept or idea of how a boyfriend / girlfriend / husband / wife should behave. They are not consistent, they change and evolve, they are never the same. They are never a particular someone. They are Life morphing and changing.

See the nature of the appearing other and know that they can not do anything other than what they do. They are limited in this play of appearances, they can not be unconditionally loving. They can not be limitless. They can not fulfil you.

Do not depend on the other to be your connection to Love. Know the Love that You are which never depends on any one else. Know that even though there appears to be someone with whom you interact, actually this is only a dance of energy.

You are absolutely alone. It is a dance with yourself. And in knowing this, there are no limits to how much you can love yourself.

"The more I give to thee, the more I have, for both are infinite."
William Shakespeare

"Let there be space in your togetherness, And let the winds of the heavens dance between you. Love one another, but make not a bond of love. Let it rather be a moving sea between the shores of your souls."
Kahlil Gibran, The Prophet

The Madness of Love

*"Whenever I'm alone with you, you make me feel like I am
whole again"*
The Cure

Here are some lines that I wrote a few years ago while I was in a
very dramatic relationship:

"You overwhelm me, you take over every thought, every
feeling, every experience.

I am not free while you are near. Even when you are far, I long
for you. What is this craziness? Is this love?

I long to ignore you. I long to be free of you. I long to behave
as if you are not there.

I long for you to go away but I know I will miss you if you do.
Is this love? Or just madness?

I enjoy you all the time. Whether it's when we are playing
together happily or whether it is in the longing for you. I enjoy
the drama of it all.

I want you out of my life! It is too painful. – but even that I
enjoy! How mad!

I seem to have a never-ending pit of longing. Not matter what
you do. It's not you.

It's the longing which I love. It is so painful, so sweet, so
addictive."

While you are in love this is a very juicy and exciting state to
be in. Your life has suddenly taken on a whole new meaning.
Everything else seems mundane in comparison to the high of
being in the dream of love. And it is a dream that is based on
needing the other to continue to play the role they are supposed
to play, otherwise you crash down to the ordinary and mundane
earth. Your lover has become your very exciting drug that you

need in order to maintain that feeling of excitement, and sense of meaning in your life. If something changes in the dream love, it can very easily flip to anger and hate. What goes up, must surely come down.... If it is a dream, then at some point you must wake up and become disappointed that life, or this love, is not as you had hoped. Then inevitably what has been felt as a blissful heaven, becomes a pit of despair and hell.

You feel intensely alive. Your existence has suddenly become meaningful because someone needs you, wants you, and makes you feel special. The feeling can become so intense that the rest of the world fades into insignificance.

However, you may also have noticed that there is a neediness and a clinging quality to that intensity. You become addicted to the other person. They have become like a drug. You are on a high when the drug is available, but even the possibility or the thought that they might no longer be there for you can lead to possessiveness, jealousy, attempts at manipulation through emotional blackmail, blaming and accusing, and more...

If the other person does leave you, this can give rise to the most intense hostility or the most profound grief and despair. In an instant, loving tenderness can turn into a savage attack or dreadful grief.

Where is the love now? Can love change into its opposite in an instant? Was it Love in the first place, or just an addictive grasping and clinging?

The drama of the cycles of love and hate makes you feel alive. It may appear that if you could only eliminate the negative or destructive cycles, then all would be well and the relationship would flower beautifully. But this is not possible.

The polarities are mutually dependent. Although the negative side of a relationship is, of course, more easily understood as dysfunctional than the positive one, you cannot have one without the other. Both are in fact different aspects of the same energy. This energy is felt as physical sensation. Highs and lows. Ups and downs. Expansion, contraction. Love, Hate.

This is the natural rhythm of life. The sensations are often felt intensely but are never understood by thought. Thought comes up with all kinds of explanations and theories, but basically it does its job of trying to make everything seem safe. It tries to hold on to things so that it is all secure and known. It comes up with stories like "You are my everything", "I can't live without you.", "I can't smile without you".

But what really seems to cause suffering is when thought makes whatever happens or whatever is experienced, mean something to me. The intense experiences of being in love and the experiences of intense pain and suffering never mean anything. Usually when we experience an intense feeling, the natural tendency of thought is to create a story about their meaning and how they affect me.

But no matter what the story, it is never true. No matter what the story, it is always a thought story. The intense experience never actually means that now this person loves me forever, or that they need to show their love in the way that I want them to. If a lover leaves you, this never means that "I am not good enough".

Although these experiences happen and the stories play out, they never refer to an actual me. They never refer to an actual individual who is in love or who suffers.

Who you are is never touched by whatever happens. All of these experiences come and go, in who you are. Sensations come and go. Thoughts come and go. Lovers come and go. But what never comes and never goes? Who you are. The Love that you are is beyond any boundaries of experience. The Love that you are is Life itself.

So the movie goes on. Life plays out as if it is all very significant and important. Sensations are felt intensely; thoughts work very hard to understand it all.

But the Love that you really are is silent. This Love does not depend on whether your lover fits the mold or whether they leave you. Love is anyway.

If you recognize the Love that you are, then you know the Love that never needs any other person or situation in order to be Love. You perhaps look to the other to find a connection with or recognition of who you are. By being loved it feels close to the Love that you know you are. If you believe you need anyone or anything (outside) in order to feel Love then this is bound to cause suffering. No one feels truly loved in a relationship of winners and losers, when both partners believe that they depend on the other for their fix. There will be a longing for freedom. Whenever a relationship involves dependency, control, sacrifice or fulfilling a particular role, it limits freedom and allows no room to breathe.

No matter how much you love and the other loves you, Love does not depend on the other. You cannot be separated from Love.

The other is not the problem. Don't wait for the other to fulfil you. In recognizing who You are, you know true fulfilment, so that when the old thought stories of being needy and insecure come up, you know that they never really refer to a needy or insecure me.

Love is the only safety and security. You do not need the other to reassure yourself of that. See the light and the dark in the play of the other. They will never be perfect and match all of your ideas of a perfect match (you would probably find them boring if they did!)

So enjoy the drama and recognize the other as a character in the movie of Love!

"Thou art to me a delicious torment."
Ralph Waldo Emerson

Wild Sensuality

"Her breath is like honey spiced with cloves,
Her mouth delicious as a ripened mango."
Srngarakarika

Everything in life is sensual and alive. Whether it's stroking the cat and feeling the texture of the fur or being in the shower and feeling the sensation of the water running over the body, listening to the rain fall outside, or the sensation of silken soft clothes against the skin ...

So often we overlook the simplicity of the simple sensations happening literally right now. We take them for granted because we want something more special.

But haven't you noticed that whenever you get that something special, which you thought you wanted, you then look for something more special than that. This is the nature of thought. It is never satisfied with what is. It will always want more. It will always find what is right now, boring, or ordinary or just too simple.

The nature of thought is to try to reach perfection and this is a never-ending task. The world will never be perfect. This character will never be perfect. There will always be an excuse to keep busy and rush around to the next task. But although there is nothing wrong with this, thought overlooks that this moment, this happening right now is already perfect just the way it is. Because it is.

In recognizing that this is the nature of thought, thought is not necessarily believed all the time. If thought says "this can't be 'it' there must be something better", this doesn't have to be believed in and followed. See that this is simply thought doing the only thing it knows to do. But what is, is still what is!

The sensation of the wind on the face, the ache of emotion in the chest, the view from the window, the sound of cars in the street, the hum of the computer, speaking on the phone, the feel of the head on a pillow....

The simple and the ordinary. Nothing to work out or understand. Nothing to know or hold on to. What 'is' goes on being what is, no matter what thought thinks! No matter how much thought seems to live in the future or the past, or stop 'me' from living in the moment, the only thing that can never be escaped from is what is.

Some traditions speak of attachment to the sensual as a problem or hindrance to Awakening. Once sensual pleasures are experienced, there is often the desire to hold on to the experience, to give it a special meaning for me and to want more and more. You may have noticed this with an experience of good food, wine or sex. The nature of thought is to try to define and own any experience. It is not the experience itself that causes suffering, but the idea that the experience can be grasped or controlled in any way.

See the nature of all experience. Whatever happens comes and goes. Everything passes. Life is sensual, but it is so alive, fresh and present, that as soon as it happens, it passes. It is too alive to be held on to. What is often held on to is only an imagination or a dead memory of a sensual experience, rather than the alive, pulsating, sensual experience itself.

Thought seems to put some kind of barrier between the person having the experience and the experience itself.

When this barrier is imagined and believed in, then this is the reality. Life can seem a little flat and dull. There can be a longing for real aliveness. Real surrender to Life. Longing for passion – to know the absolute sensuality of Life. Longing to surrender without restriction. But thought puts up the barrier of separation, fear and control.

When this imaginary barrier is no longer believed in, it may still come up but it is simply not believed in. It is seen for what it is. Simply thought doing its job and trying to make things safe. Then there is no experiencer and only the experience. No one claiming the experience as mine and no one with any idea that they can control what happens – an absolute surrender to whatever is. Surrender to wild sensuality!

Then nature comes alive. There is intimacy with all that is, in just the way that it is already. Look at water. It ripples with light and darkness. It is magic stuff. We take it so for granted when we turn on the tap and have a shower or drink a glass of it. But look at it shine. Feel the sensation of it on the body. Stand near a lake or river and feel the calm that it creates. Isn't it amazing how being near to this magic liquid can create such a feeling?

Look at a field of corn swaying in the wind. So bursting with life. Look at an office full of people – all busy being very important people! Just the very fact that everything exists at all is an absolute miracle. Not only does it exist, but it is so exploding with life energy, so sensual and rich. Sometimes just looking at a thing of beauty like a flower, or the stars, this can trigger a rush of bliss sensation.

Meditation or other kinds of practices can trigger this too. Or even drugs. Sometimes there doesn't seem to be any trigger at all. You never know when the body will be touched or respond to a situation in a physical expression. Sometimes the responses are socially accepted or appropriate for the situation and sometimes not. The body can explode with laughter at a funeral and cry at a party. It does not always fit into what you might think is a good idea or appropriate for the circumstances.

I often experience a rush of sensation when I'm listening to music. Sometimes I am so touched that I notice tears pouring down my face. At times I listen to music on the train and I wear sunglasses to avoid people asking if I'm ok! I have cried during a fire drill, giggled in a very serious meeting.

The body is often touched by watching a beautiful scene in nature, perhaps a river or a flower. Sensations and emotions seem to burst out and can not be contained. The experience of falling in love is a sensual, gorgeous expression of the Love that You are beyond all experience. When you get a taste of this Love, it usually comes with such a rush or feeling of a high that nothing else matters. The sensations and emotions in the body are intense and often so blissful that people sacrifice anything for it.

But like any drug when this bliss fades or changes to some other sensation, you long for more bliss... This longing is an intense sensual experience in itself. It is felt as a physical sensation as well as emotional. See that you actually love to long. You love to miss someone or to long for spiritual awakening. It is the longing that feels so alive. It fills all the senses, just as a sexual experience might.

Sexual energy is not restricted to what you think about it. It bursts out when you least expect it. If there is an openness to Life, then where are the boundaries? I fall in love with lots of people all the time. Love does not care about who you think you should fall in love with. Although it does not mean that you necessarily act on it, sexual energy is often felt when you least expect. Sexual energy is not something to be controlled or dealt with.

It is not something that is right or wrong. It is absolutely ordinary and yet absolutely extra-ordinary. Simply see the nature of it. It is life force. It Aliveness felt physically. Sexual energy, with its fusion of love, play and ecstasy, is Life celebrating Life. Everything is sensual and sexual. Life pulsating in whatever happens. Merging, separating, merging, separating.... Coming and going, feeling, sensing, vibrating, tingling...

"Isn't the secret intent of this great Earth, when it forces lovers together, that inside their boundless emotion, all things may shudder with joy?"
Rainer Maria Rilke, The Enlightened Heart

Unconditional Love and Compassion

"I will always love you. No matter what you do, what you say,
no matter what I do or say."
The Cure

There seems to be a tremendous amount of confusion around the words 'compassion' and 'unconditional love'. They have become infused with ideas of how you should behave. Thought very sweetly tries to create what it thinks is right and good. Perhaps we think that unconditional love means that you should try to love people without judging them. You should try to accept them just as they are.

Compassion is understood to mean that you should try to be kind and self-sacrificing towards others. To love them as you love yourself. But have you tried that? Theoretically it sounds like a good idea and obviously these kinds of ideas and behaviour seem better than ideas of hurting others or being selfish and causing suffering.

However, if you are trying to modify your behaviour to suit your ideas of what you think is right or wrong, it will sometimes feel unnatural or like an uphill struggle and in fact impossible to do. You may notice that there are times when you do not or can not behave according to your ideas – Life shows you that experience can not be fitted into the mould of what you think. Life is wild and free and not always what you may think it should be.

"Compassion is ruthless. It pulls the rug out from under your feet."
Dolano

Jesus taught his followers not only to love their neighbours but also their enemies. Buddha taught the practise of compassion towards all creatures and various new age teachers suggest visualising peace and love in the world. There is a Buddhist practise whereby you first practise loving yourself, then a benefactor, then a friend, then someone neutral, and then an enemy. To love someone with whom you have an unresolved conflict is said to be the door from conditional love to unconditional love. Compassion or loving kindness is distinguished from passion or desire. Passion and desire are seen to be a delusion which masquerades as love. This kind of love is understood to be limited only to experiences of pleasure to the exclusion of pain or ugliness.

While there is a belief in separation, there will be a belief in the duality of right and wrong, good and bad. Some thoughts and actions will be considered to fall in one category rather than the other. While these attitudes and practises may make you feel good for a while, they never seem to last very long.

The pendulum of polarity naturally swings the opposite way eventually no matter how compassionate you try to be. You can practice compassion all day but then when someone accidentally bumps into you or stands on your toe, you may well swear and feel hatred towards them. This then may well provoke guilty feelings that you have not been compassionate towards them.

It is a never-ending struggle of trying to replace so-called negative thoughts and actions with positive ones. Trying to be compassionate and unconditionally loving can also often be a great ego-trip. You feel so special and worthy because you are being such a great person. You have a very special identity as a good or kind person.

In fact, the truth is that you have no identity, therefore there is no need to try to become a better person. You are not any kind of person. You have no quality and every quality.

Often these practices are the mind's way of trying to replicate the qualities of the Unconditional Love and Compassion which You are already. For most people their true longing is to manifest unconditional Love in their daily life – to live as Love. And so, mind innocently, tries to do this.

We practise compassion and try to be good and loving and open our heart. And perhaps with persistent practise, these qualities do seem to manifest more and more. But this is a never-ending path of trying to align who you think you are, and all the qualities which you think you have, with that which has no quality.

You don't even know all the qualities which you need to perfect. There seem to be continually more qualities depending on layers of thought that are seemingly penetrated through practise. What You are is already all the qualities that you desire and in simply recognizing that and giving up any trying, I notice that these qualities are manifested in their own way.

These teachings about unconditional love and compassion, essentially point to the way it is already, but they are often interpreted to mean that you should try to modify your behaviour or thinking. Unconditional Love is a recognition, not a practice. If you recognize once and for all that there is no separation, then there is no question of separation between yourself, a friend or an enemy.

There may well be conflicts with others but this is always seen to be a meaningless dance of energy. There is never any real problem or love lost. Whether it is passion, desire or acts of compassion, any kind of belief that any of these things have more or less value or importance or mean anything to me, is a delusion.

You are already absolute Compassion without ever needing to be compassionate. True Compassion is the truth of actual experience. No need to define it or to pretend that things are other than the way they are. Who You are is all inclusive Compassion. It never excludes pain or ugliness. Compassion does not mean that you need to behave in a self-less manner. Compassion is not reserved only for others. It is for whatever happens, including and not separate from, what happens for yourself.

If anger, hatred, anxiety or desire happens, it happens. It does not need to be fixed or changed. This is Acceptance beyond any trying to accept. Seeing the way it is already. Seeing that You are all that is. There are no boundaries.

This is Love. Recognize the unconditional Love that You are already and know that no matter what happens, unconditional Love is anyway. Love does not depend on the temporary experience of feeling loving. Love does not depend on the temporary experience of being in love with someone. Love does not depend on the temporary experience of being kind or nice.

Know true unconditional Love and then there is no need to try to behave that way. Know true Compassion and then see that you never need to try to be compassionate. This is radical. If you recognize who You really are, you know that there are no conditions and no limitations to the Love that You are.

"Compassion... is not the all-glorious compassion of loving a million people in a far distant land. It is the nitty-gritty compassion of being at ease with the things that we experience whether or not they are to our liking. True loving-kindness isn't a construction of a thought or a feeling. It is the ability to be present with experience on a moment to moment basis with awareness. Loving kindness is awareness."
A Theravardan Buddhist nun

Conditional Love

"Love is patient and kind; love is not jealous, or conceited, or proud; love is not ill-mannered, or selfish, or irritable; love does not keep a record of wrongs: love is not happy with evil, but is happy with the truth. Love never gives up: its faith, hope and patience never fail. Love is eternal."
1 Corinthians 13

True Love is not dependent on any condition. But the experience of love is often conditional and based in egotistical conditions, demands and expectations. "Do what I want and I will love you. Become who I want you to be and I will love you."

Conditional love means that we give and receive love and approval only if we are good and well behaved by certain standards. Only the nice parts are acceptable. We hide all the not-so-nice emotions and desires. The longer this goes on the more lonely and 'disconnected' we feel and long to know the Love that simply is no matter what the condition. No wonder - if you reaffirm the separateness it will feel painful.

Just as when you reaffirm the oneness it feels good. Usually relationships seem to be based in conditional love. "I love you because you are compatible with me." "I love you because you are my daughter." "I love you because you love me."

Love seems to be confined to this particular relationship and is bound by this particular definition. Ideas of what we think this love means, define our relationship. "If you love me, you should always be nice to me." "If you love me, you should always respect what I say."

It seems that relationships work well when both people have the same or similar idea of what their love means. This feels safe and secure and logically understood.

But the trouble with any definition of love, is that Love is wild and free! It does not fit into any boundaries or definitions. Every expression, every smile, every laugh it is all expressing the lightness and Love which You are. None of it can be contained. It bursts out in an explosion of Life.

Whilst you try hard to make love fit into an idea you will no doubt feel the contradiction of it all. You will feel the pain of separation. So no matter how safe it may feel, eventually you may need to break free of it in one way or another.

Seeking love and approval actually means you are confirming its absence. If you are searching for love from someone else to fulfil you, you are actually saying that you are not already whole. You are confirming that you need the other to know yourself as being whole. You depend on the other to know the Love that You are.

Trying to be good stems from a dualistic way of thinking about what is good and bad, and implies that you are not good enough already. It fuels self-righteousness, seeing someone as right or wrong and essentially separation. If you don't trust that you are already Love itself, then you may well believe that you need thought to tell you how to behave or to be your compass in life. But thought splits everything into good and bad, right and wrong, this way or that way. The Love that is, is absolute wholeness and is never divided, ever. Whatever is, is neither good nor bad, right nor wrong, it is simply what it is.

Needing other people's love or approval seems to prevent you from trusting what you know beyond that. You fear breaking the rules and being totally lost. Really standing alone in what you know to be true can feel very frightening. It takes courage to not know which way to go, or how to be. Rules and conditions can feel easier to just go along with.

These rules and conditions are not only towards others, but also towards yourself. Most of the time you love yourself only when you behave well. When you do something wrong, you are treated with disdain. Thought blames myself and hates myself. But trying to love myself with positive thoughts or affirmations is only a temporary plaster.

Only seeing that what I am is already Love, can this character be as awful as it might be and, radically, I am Love despite it all. This recognition of Love itself, actually seems to nourish the character and it often seems to gain confidence and flourish. Love sees no separation, no difference between one thing and another. My lover or a worm. Love simply loves. Love is not dutiful. Love is light, liberating and expansive. Love is wild.

We are not fallen angels who need to repent or stop thinking. We don't need to purify ourselves. It is not a battle against self-indulgent destructive impulses.

Life plays at whatever happens and it is all included in Love without conditions. Everything is good and right, because it is.

Hate

What is Hate? We have a lot of inhibitions and ideas about the meaning of this word. There are almost as many interpretations of this word as the word Love. In polite company people tend to be scared of using this word. It seems such a strong emotion with so much finality involved. Once you say you hate something or someone, there is not more room for discussion. It is final. It is so different to saying "I find that irritating" or even "I don't like you".

It is like a sword cutting through all thought or all other possible considerations. This is why it is used so sparingly by most people. They are scared to end things once and for all. They want to leave a door open for more possibilities, for more drama, for more thought. Scared to let go of the drama of thought to cut through to what is absolutely final right now.

It sounds strange to talk about hate in a book about Love because we usually think of hate as being an extension of anger and other strong so-called negative emotions. And of course it often is like this. But I am talking about the hate which is as final as real Love. The end of all discussion and reasoning. Simply what is right now. Of course often people hate because of a feeling of anger and a story of injustice. But without referring to the anger and the story of injustice, the hate itself is still final. It is absolute. It is full and total.

I'm not suggesting that you should go around hating everything and everyone but in that total hate, there is absolute relaxation. Everything is let go of. All logic and reasoning is relinquished. By hating someone completely, we let go of the story around them and lose them totally.

When this ownership is over, then all that is left is Love. You have never been separate from them. The Love that You are is what they are.

Hate is the ultimate honesty. Thought always finds reasons to hate – a look, an annoying habit or behaviour. Most of the time we try to suppress these feelings because we think that we should be nice and tolerant. But secretly we are burning with this hatred underneath. Because hate is so often misinterpreted or taken personally, we are reluctant to use it. Hate jumps beyond the personal. But really we would love to say there and then "I hate the way you just looked at me!" There doesn't need to be any anger expressed. The anger only develops when it is not expressed. There is no blame in hate. No fingers are pointed to someone else. It is simply an expression there and then. I'm not suggesting that you now say "I hate…" all the time. Simply that you see hate for what it is, and no longer fear it.

When you can do this, already there is a freedom and clarity about it. Hate is as valid an expression as Love. So-called negative emotions come and go as do positive emotions. Love is Hate. Hate is Love. The beginning and the end. This is Life. Life flows in both extremes. Empty is full. Full is empty. Both are the same. Both are one.

Why hate Hate and love Love? Why not love Hate and hate Love? When you look beyond the concepts of both hate or love, you know that there are no positive or negative emotions or experiences. When there is a feeling of hate, there is no problem or reason to try to change things. It is seen to be simply what is happening. While it is happening there is no escape from it, and so why fight it? The fight is only more confusion and wriggling. It will pass when it passes and is simply like a cloud in the sky. It does not always need to be expressed, but simply noticing that Hate is felt now, is already a freedom. Love loves Hate too. This is already the end of the struggle.

Gradual Dis-Integration

"When you stop trying to improve yourself, Life starts to improve you.
Life gently caresses you"
Osho

What a paradox! There is only life happening right now with nothing ever needing to be more, or different to this. Love simply is. Nothing is needed or lacking. However, paradoxically there is a gradual integration of this into the daily living of the apparent individual. This is not an integration of an idea or belief, this is living as Love. Recognize death and then live as Love. Know who you really are and then when Life is seen for the truth of what it really is, then the truth of every thought, emotion or experience is also unveiled.

Since this is not an expression of a belief system or philosophy, it is simply not enough to agree theoretically that your true nature is Love. What you really long for is to no longer live in fear, to live as Love totally, and to know this absolutely in every moment. There is no end to the integration of this recognition. Life surprises itself with ever more situations and circumstances whereby there may be a playing out of separation or fear, only to be seen in the light of the Love that is aware of itself.

Before this recognition, you may have believed that you as a separate individual could do something to open your heart or be true to yourself. You may have gone to courses or workshops to learn how to be more vulnerable and reveal your true feelings.

Actually once you recognize that there is no separate individual who can control or, in fact, to do anything, it becomes obvious that things work in the opposite way around to what you believed before. You believed that by trying hard to open your heart or meditating to become aware of the mind, you would arrive at the final goal, but actually in recognizing who You really are, which is the final goal, opening your heart, being more vulnerable in relationships, becoming more aware of thought and emotion, simply happens by itself. You never need to try to do this. But there is a noticing that it all happens gradually. No one trying to do it, and yet it happens like a flow of energy.

Many spiritual traditions teach a path or a process which leads towards the final goal of freedom. What I am saying is the opposite. The final goal of freedom is right here, right now. Realize that absolutely, and then see the process of disintegration begin.

I say disintegration because it is a falling apart and collapsing of all belief systems and held concepts, all old patterns of behaving and relating. This is really losing everything. In recognizing who you really are, there is a leap beyond everything that you have ever held sacred, serious and meaningful, but then this losing everything goes on and on and on... Forever freefalling. Whenever a thought, or emotion, or situation comes up, there is a seeing, as if for the first time, that this too is simply a flow of energy or a sensation happening in emptiness, and never means anything to me. All reference points are lost again and again...

On the one hand there is no gradual integration in time because there is only Absolute Presence and by the very nature of Presence, there is nothing outside of this moment. And yet, in time, there does seem to be a gradual integration of this recognition of Presence. Waking up to who you really are is recognized once and for all, but then the nature of thought is that it knows only to live in time and separation.

Living the recognition of timeless, limitless Love, despite thought's insistence on the opposite, can seem to require a certain courage moment to moment. As every experience or thought happens, there is the courage to see that there is nothing to hold on to, again and again. There is never a resting place in anything that happens. Not this thought, not this experience... Nothing that ever happens defines who I am. Realizing again and again, that I don't know.

This is not a practise of trying to be aware of whatever happens, because no trying is necessary. Once you recognize that there is no separate me with any power or volition to try to be aware, then it is obvious that there is a natural unfolding that happens. Once you have seen the light, everything that comes up after that is gradually seen in the light of this recognition.

It is a gradual revealing of each and every trick of thought, every game of a so-called ego, every owning and manipulating, every story of me and my pain and suffering is uncovered and revealed to be the farce that it is. Nothing that happens is ever assumed to be owned by me. However, there can still be a playing out of old patterns as if there is a me that is believed in. These old stories or patterns, are played out and are either seen for what they are or not.

It seems that sometimes, their illusory nature is seen immediately, but often these stories can come up again and again before they are truly burnt up in the light of the Love that you really are. It never matters if these stories or patterns play out forever. Nothing ever means anything. No matter what happens, it never means that you have lost anything. But in contrast to who you really are, any movement from an imaginary me or ego, is known to be a pretence and is often felt as constricting and physically painful.

Who you thought you were slowly disintegrates... until all you are is this sensation.

> *"Since love grows within you, so beauty grows.*
> *For love is the beauty of the soul."*
> **St. Augustine**

The Wrong Way Around!

"You are always in love and you can only love yourself,
the Changeless One in which even space is.
There is no beginning, no middle, and no end to it.
Only love is worth loving and this is your own Self."
H.W.L Poonja (Papaji)

Most teachings are trying to replicate the Love that you are. This is still a denial that you are that already, just the way you are right now. By suggesting that you should try to be more loving, or more aware, you are believing that who you already are is not already all that you try to become. You can not try to be Love when you already are Love. There is no need to try.

Most teachings and traditions teach of a path leading to a final goal of enlightenment or fulfilment. On the path you must work hard to perfect yourself in whatever way that particular teaching suggests.

You must learn not to be attached, you must learn to open your heart, you must learn to control the mind, you must learn not to react in a way which is based in past conditioning.... But all this is rooted in the idea that you are in control of your life, as well as the idea that precisely the way it is, is not good enough.

This is all the wrong way around. Once you recognize who you really are, then everything else takes care of itself. Then you see that who you really are is never attached and is always an open heart.

The mind never needs to be controlled because it is obvious that it never disturbs anyone and it is clear that there is no past conditioning because who you really are is absolute Presence. There has never been a past for conditioning to happen.

In this recognition there is a general relaxation. This is the end of seeking. A great relief. In this relaxation, slowly things take care of themselves.

Because thought is always free to chatter and never needs to be quiet, it is also free to relax and be quieter. With this recognition there is more and more opening in Love which is revealed in the individual's life, without it ever needing to happen. A surrender to Life itself which expresses itself freely as whatever happens. No one standing in the way any more. No one in control of anything.

In fact the search for enlightenment or Love is really the search to align this play of appearances with that that knows the play.

People strive to be good, to be kind, to be meditative and to love and be loved because they already know the Love that they are and there is the search to find it in this expression. So when people dedicate their lives to a spiritual search they are surrendering everything in order to align their lives with truth.

But in recognizing that what I am is truth already, it is obvious that there is no need to try to align my life with truth. Life happens out of control without any effort or trying. In recognizing who I am there is a natural expression of that in everything. So it works the other way around. Gently, slowly, naturally there is the play of more and more clarity and expression of Love.

Who You are is Love and Freedom already and never needs embodying or expressing, and yet this play goes on. Once there is a recognition of who you really are, Love reveals itself more and more. But it happens out of control. So that this apparent journey of life becomes a beautiful unveiling as life situations present themselves. It never stops. What would be the pleasure in living if it was not ever-expanding and surprising?

After recognizing who you are, the path does not actually stop, it just becomes playful and less serious. It is no longer about me and where I am heading, but about how Life expresses and experiences.

We believe that we need to work on ourselves to be free but actually it's the other way around. Recognize who you are first and then everything falls into place gently and slowly.

Slowly this Love that you are, unfolds and reveals itself in this life. In recognizing the Emptiness that you are, you know that there is no one who ever needs try to modify their behaviour, there is no one who even cares about their behaviour, and yet bizarrely, you notice that behaviour and interactions can't help but be more and more infected with Love.

So Why Love Less Than Totally?

"Love... is the only teacher that keeps us on our knees all the time."
Adyashanti

Why love less than totally? Why hold back? What are you waiting for? No one is going to come along one day and finally give you permission to love now! Are you going to wait for death? Will you die without ever having loved totally? Why are you putting it off for even one moment more?

Awakening or recognizing who You truly are is a bridge. It is the seeming bridge between a doing and an undoing. Before this recognition it seems that you must do everything you can to try to wake up. In recognizing who you really are, you realize that you have never done anything in your life.

The experience of awakening or a glimpse of absolute Presence or Love, is the bridge. So often you get confused and believe that it is the experience itself which is special, but the experience is only the bridge. You must cross to the other side and leave all bridges behind. Dive into the Love that you already are, and drown.

Love is only right now. Total surrender to Life, to Love. There is only absolute surrender right now. It's already happening. Life is already in love with itself. Love is recognized, not practiced. Love is not a doing. It is an un-doing. You are un-done in Love. Unravelled. Love is nakedness. Love is Presence which is totally unguarded.

The nature of Love is to expand and open. It is thought which seems to diminish Love, but Love never diminishes. Love is forever expanding in this expression of Life. Any thought story or restriction, any tension or old habits are burnt up in the fire of ever-present Love. This can often be very uncomfortable and challenging, which is why most people try to do anything to avoid standing naked in this fire. Love is not always comfortable. Love is not always nice.

Love is wild and free. You love it and you hate it. You long for it and you run from it, because you know it will destroy you.

Know the Love that You are and no longer put ideas of who you think you are or what you think you know, before Love, no matter what idea, even the idea of Love.

Even the idea of forgetting to Love. You can never forget Love, because you can never remember Love. You can never have any idea of Love. Love is not a certain attitude or behaviour. I'm not suggesting you purposely change your behaviour to be in line with your ideas of what Love looks like. Thought can not do this.

Love is already the openness into which you are opening. Love is already all that thought thinks you should become. Love is revealed in every form, behaviour or thought. Love is total openness to whatever is, as it is.

Love despite fear. Love despite what the thought story says. Thought will hear this message as something that you should do. But I am not pointing out your deficiency. I am not telling you to be more loving in your life. I am saying that you are already all that you long to be. Language is not sufficient to express this. Words can only say one thing at a time. Love is an alive paradox. You are an alive paradox.

Love goes on forever expanding and burning all restriction and contraction. There is no final state where all is known once and for all. Love loves expanding.

If you believe that you have arrived somewhere or have found some permanent state, this is simply arrogance. Love is never found. Thought wants a resting place, but there is none. Thought wants something to hold on to, but there is none. Thought may say "I've got it!" or "I am awakened now", "I am enlightened now", but Love can not be contained by thought. Love doesn't care what thought says.

Love goes on and on and on destroying you...

For further information about
Meeting in Not-Knowing with Unmani,
and to contact the author,
please visit:

www.not-knowing.com

BOOKS

O is a symbol of the world, of oneness and unity. In different cultures it also means the "eye," symbolizing knowledge and insight. We aim to publish books that are accessible, constructive and that challenge accepted opinion, both that of academia and the "moral majority."

Our books are available in all good English language bookstores worldwide. If you don't see the book on the shelves ask the bookstore to order it for you, quoting the ISBN number and title. Alternatively you can order online (all major online retail sites carry our titles) or contact the distributor in the relevant country, listed on the copyright page.

See our website **www.o-books.net** for a full list of over 500 titles, growing by 100 a year.

And tune in to myspiritradio.com for our book review radio show, hosted by June-Elleni Laine, where you can listen to the authors discussing their books.